The RFU Rugby Union Referee's Manual

Richard Greensted
Second edition

RUGBY
FOOTBALL
UNION

A&C Black • London

Second edition published 2004 by
A & C Black Publishers Ltd
37 Soho Square, London W1D 3QZ
www.acblack.com

First edition 1997
Second edition 2004

ISBN 0 7136 6740 0

A CIP catalogue record for this book
is available from the British Library.

Acknowledgments
Cover photograph © Empics
Textual photographs © Empics
The Referee Signals in Appendix 1 are reproduced courtesy of the IRB © IRB

This book has been typeset in Goudy
Printed and bound in Great Britain by Biddles Ltd., King's Lynn

Contents

Foreword

The game of rugby has had to contend with many changes in a short space of time. As referees, we have needed to keep pace with these changes. Many training programmes have been introduced to help facilitate the modern game.

As part of this initiative, I am delighted that the RFU has now produced a manual for referees. This manual gives referees an excellent insight into what is expected of them, as well as offering sound practical advice and support on all aspects of refereeing.

At the same time, the manual will assist in accelerating the development of new referees and will also act as a very useful reference point for even the most experienced referee.

I'm convinced that regular reading of this manual will enhance the performance of any referee, allowing all participants - referees and players alike - to maximise their enjoyment of this wonderful game.

Ed Morrison
Former RFU Panel of National Referees, International referee and 1995 Rugby World Cup final referee.

Author's note

Inevitably, the production of this manual has depended heavily on the wisdom, advice and counsel of many people.

I would especially like to thank Steve Griffiths, who gave much guidance and encouragement; Keith Bonser, who added valuable commentary on the players' perspective; Jimmy Crowe, who dealt swiftly and constructively with questions of Law; and Ian Dorrn, a good friend who has always been ready to listen and help.

I also want to thank everyone at the Metropolitan Surrey Society of Rugby Football Referees: without their excellent training, commitment and dedication, I would not have been able to write this book.

Two final points to note.

(1) This manual is based on the Laws for the 2004–5 season.

(2) As we all know, an increasing number of women are becoming referees. For the purposes of style I have used the masculine form throughout the book, but all such references apply equally to women.

Richard Greensted

CHAPTER 1

Why be a referee?

You've just watched a rugby match. Perhaps it was at your local club; perhaps one of your children was playing at school or in a mini-rugby tournament; or perhaps it was the climax of the Five Nations Championship. But now you're saying to yourself: 'I could do that. I could be a referee. That looks fun!'

So what do you do next? What sort of person becomes a referee, and what's involved once you get started? This manual aims to tell you what you need to know about referceing - before, during and after the actual match. By the time you've finished reading this book, you should have a very clear idea of whether you've got what it takes - although nobody really knows that until they've run out on to the pitch with a whistle in their pocket. Existing referees may also learn something useful from this book, as it never does any harm to confirm your understanding of the skills involved.

The scenario above is just one of the motivations for becoming a referee. Rugby is a sport which encourages and welcomes participation at all levels, from playing, refereeing and administration to serving the post-match teas. It's a sport which is still primarily played for fun, in spite of the advent of the open game. On chilly Saturday afternoons friendly matches are played the length and breadth of the country, with no rewards available other than the satisfaction of having enjoyed 80 minutes of rugby. For the game to work at this level, there must be an abundant and continuing supply of volunteers - and referees are volunteers you must have if a match is going to be played. Without a referee you can't have a match.

Typically, rugby referees have been drawn from the pool of ex-players. Players who have reached a certain age, or who have had to retire due to injury, work or family commitments, can still participate as referees, and will be providing a vital service to the game if they do. But it isn't just ex-players with cauliflower ears and broken noses who aspire to refereeing; the motivation to become a rugby referee stems from a number of different sources.

Whilst giving something back to the game is clearly a major factor, there are other reasons for taking up the whistle.

- To help to raise the standard of refereeing.
- To contribute to players' enjoyment of the game.
- To keep fit and active.
- To stay in touch with the game.
- Most importantly, to enjoy it.

Whatever the motivation, there is a place for you in the game. Referees are not born, they are made. There is no single type of person who is the perfect referee: they come from all walks of life, and they all have their idiosyncrasies and foibles. In fact, refereeing is very much like playing: it doesn't matter where you come from, or who you are, as long as you can perform on the pitch.

The tools of the trade

Some will say that refereeing is an art, some a science - but it is neither. Refereeing is a skill and, like any other skill, it can be taught and learnt. Most referees are only limited by their personal ambitions and aspirations: if they want to get to the top, and they're good enough, they will. But there are characteristics which the referee needs to have if he is to succeed.

Firstly, he needs to have an **empathy** with the game. It is difficult, but not impossible, to referee a rugby match if you don't have some intrinsic understanding of, and feeling for, the game. After all, you are planning to go out there and look after 30 players for 80 minutes: if you don't understand what they're trying to achieve, and you can't differentiate between positive and negative play, you're going to get into trouble. This is why ex-players have a headstart when it comes to refereeing. But knowing the game from the players' perspective isn't enough, and can sometimes put you at a disadvantage: the skill of refereeing is so different, and requires such altered levels of concentration, fitness and positioning, that recently retired players can easily find themselves in a mess early on in their refereeing career. It takes time to adjust to the new demands.

Secondly, the successful referee will be a good **communicator**. Later in this book we will look at the subject of communication in some depth, but it's important to understand that the rugby referee, as distinct from many other sports, talks and signals almost constantly during a match. The players need the referee to tell them what he expects from them, and what he is looking for. In this respect, the referee acts in a preventive capacity, advising players on what course of action to take so that they do not infringe. This is not cheating, and it is not contrary to the spirit or the Laws of the game: referees are positively encouraged to develop these communication skills so that games under their control are well managed and enjoyable for the players.

Thirdly, the referee must be **fit**. Fitness is obviously relative, but you need to be able to keep up with play, to change pace and direction quickly, to recover rapidly, and to have enough in reserve that you can still make good decisions.

These three elements make up the base requirement for a rugby referee, and they could all be listed under the heading of **management** skills. Managing a match is not simply blowing the whistle when an infringement occurs and keeping the score and time. Match management encompasses empathy, communication, and fitness, as well as knowledge of the Laws. You have to know the Laws: some are more important than others, but they all need to be learnt and, more critically, understood. What are the motivations for each Law? What are they trying to achieve? How should they be interpreted? Knowing the answers to questions such as these is part of the skill of refereeing. When managing a match, it is essential that the referee remembers that the safety of the players is the most important element during all phases of the game.

Help is at hand

So rugby refereeing is a challenge, not a soft option. That challenge can only be met if you are properly prepared and fully confident. Fortunately, there is a huge infrastructure in place to support you, train you, encourage you, and develop you. Referees carry a large burden of responsibility, and they are not expected to shoulder this alone. In fact, the Foreword to the Laws actually states that: *It is the duty of Unions to ensure that the Game at every level is conducted in accordance with disciplined and sporting behaviour. This principle cannot be upheld solely by the referee; its observance also rests on Unions, affiliated bodies and clubs.* The game is on your side from the word 'go'; volunteer to become a referee and you will immediately benefit from the combined support of administrators, players and coaches. The game needs referees, and fully recognises their importance.

Most referees start out with their local Referee Society. They may have done a couple of 'Extra B' XV games at their club to help out but, as likely as not, they will have no real experience of refereeing. Few will ever have seen a Law book, let alone have read it! Referee Societies are locally organised, and are administered by current and former referees. Although these Societies are entirely separate from the game's central and regional administrators, they act in close co-operation with them. The principle of most Societies is that they organise referee resources on behalf of the clubs they serve, for which they are paid a fee by those clubs to cover their costs. Their primary function is to allocate referees to club fixtures; as an additional service, they organise training and development of their member referees, teachers, and club referees. Comprehensive training and development programmes are provided to the Societies by the RFU Referee Department.

Joining a Society is pretty painless and is usually free. It need not commit you to refereeing: many Societies organise and run open days for potential referees so that they can get a feel of what's involved and the commitment that's required. If you're still keen, you can join and ease your way into refereeing. But, as with everything else in life, if you really want to know what's involved, you've got to do it for yourself. Getting a match and refereeing it, however intimidating that may sound, is the only true way to tell whether it's for you. No-one will be upset if you discover that it isn't - but you're more likely to be pleasantly surprised! There's more about Societies and their work in Chapter 5.

Hopes and dreams

It is easy, and perfectly understandable, to be intimidated by the concept of refereeing. If you come in to the game with little knowledge of the Laws, and even less experience, it can seem like a fairly daunting task. Suddenly you are required to know the Laws intimately - something that is not necessary for players - and you are no longer part of the playing fraternity: you are the classic poacher turned gamekeeper. You may be concerned about how players, coaches and spectators will treat you, and whether you will be blamed for everything that goes wrong on the pitch. But, whilst it's true that you need a thick skin to be a good referee, it's also true that, if you do your job well and are consistent and fair, you will earn the respect of players. Unlike some other sports, there is no 'them and us' mentality in rugby: players and coaches appreciate the contribution of a good referee and will be quite happy to discuss your performance with you in the bar after the match. If you think of yourself as the 31st player on the pitch, it will give you much more confidence about your role as a referee.

You will also find that the same concerns, hopes and fears are shared by all rugby referees, however senior they may be. One of the great things about the game is that you, as a trainee referee, can be sitting in the club changing room with very senior referees with years of experience, and they will gladly share that experience with you. You need only ask: there's no such thing as a stupid question when it comes to refereeing! Every referee started the same way, and they all remember only too well how puzzling it can all be at the beginning.

The other beauty of refereeing is that you are able to go as far as you want. When you start you may have dreams of ending up as a World Cup Final referee and, if you're good enough, you'll be in contention. But all participants in the game realise that it is not just World Cup referees who are needed: it is equally important to have a dedicated corps of referees who will handle the more junior games, those men and women who will happily turn out each week for friendlies. The game is built on these foundations - and, of course, the top players work their way through the ranks in exactly the same way as referees. At whatever level you choose to participate, you are providing an invaluable service. Even if you can only turn out once a month, that is one more fixture which will benefit from a qualified referee, and 30 more satisfied players. The business of refereeing is both democratic and pragmatic.

The game needs you

Refereeing is rather like golf. When you start, you wonder what all the fuss is about because it seems so easy. But, as you progress, you realise that it is an incredibly challenging exercise, and you can never relax or rest on your laurels. You learn to be more critical of your own performance, and you start to focus on the areas that need your attention rather than the things you know you can do well. It becomes addictive and, in your determination to improve, you set ever higher standards. You never stop learning, and you never stop needing the advice and coaching of others.

With all the changes that have taken place in rugby over the past few years, there is a growing requirement for qualified referees. Sadly, there are still too many fixtures for the Referee Societies to cover, although a lot of work has been done to bring new referees into the sport. The game of rugby is not just what you see on television - the internationals and the national leagues and cups - but the thousands of matches played throughout the country every week. If the game is to improve, many more qualified referees have to be found so that players can perform to their full potential.

So the answer to the title of this chapter - 'Who'd be a referee?' - is simple: people like you. You're reading this, which means that you have some interest in finding out more. Whatever your background, there's probably a place for you in the game, and there are certainly plenty of people who will help you to find it. You only have to ask.

The purpose of this book is to give you some advice on how to become a better referee. By itself, reading the book will not improve your performance, but it will help you to understand what's required. You have to put the theory into practice, and you'll find that it's well worth the effort - refereeing is far more enjoyable if you know what you're doing!

CHAPTER 2

The principles of management

Rugby is a game that encompasses a fascinating mixture of differing skills and demands. It is about power, strength, endurance, agility and speed, qualities which are nowadays required from all players, regardless of their position. The Laws have been adapted to encourage and reward these attributes, and coaches have recognised the need to develop new skills in their players to meet the challenge.

Rugby is a flexible and versatile sport. It can be played in a variety of ways, and no two matches will ever be the same. For the referee, each match will contain critical phases and elements that must be monitored and managed effectively for both players and spectators to get the maximum enjoyment from the contest.

Management and communication are the key skills that the referee uses to enhance the game. Technical aspects of the game will be dealt with later.

1 The role of the referee

The Foreword to the Laws states: *The Object of the Game is that two teams of 15, ten or seven players each, observing fair play according to the Laws and a sporting spirit, should by carrying, passing, kicking and grounding the ball score as many points as possible, the team scoring the greater number of points to be the winner of the match. The Laws of the Game ... are complete and contain all that is necessary to enable the game to be played correctly and fairly. It is the duty of the referee to apply fairly the Laws of the Game without any variation or omission.*

Put like that, the role of the referee seems pretty straightforward. In practice, however, things aren't quite that simple. The referee faces a series of challenges and must have the necessary skills to apply fundamental principles to his management of the match. What is the precise role of the referee, and what should the players expect from him? The referee acts in conjunction with others to promote these principles.

1.1 The referee as game manager

No matter what the level, there is one primary objective for the referee: **to manage an environment in which two sides can play and enjoy a match of rugby football safely within the Laws of the game**.

How do you set about the task of achieving that objective? As the 31st participant in the match, the referee plays a pivotal role - yet no-one goes to a match to watch the referee. In fact, the best compliment that can be paid to a referee is to hear it said: 'What a wonderful match that was!' By association, the referee can't have done a bad job. As a manager, the referee needs to be in control and to exercise his skills without overpowering the action, unobtrusively creating that special environment in which good rugby can be played and enjoyed safely.

The role of the referee is to create a situation which allows the participants to play to the best of their ability. The referee cannot make people play well, but he can give them the time and space to do so through his management. There is nothing more frustrating than to referee a match in which the players continually fail to make the best of their chances: it is only human nature to feel that you as the referee have also failed in some way. Good referees know that they will not always be able to improve the standard of a match. As long as they have made every effort to create and sustain the right conditions, there is nothing more that can be asked of them.

The referee is therefore a manager. He knows the theory and purpose of the Laws, and on the pitch it is his duty to apply and interpret those Laws for the proper management of the match. He is also a facilitator. At the most basic level, his presence allows the two teams to play, but there is much more to it than that. By applying his skill, knowledge and experience, the referee gives the players an opportunity to perform to the best of their abilities. The Law of Advantage helps the referee to allow continuity, and a good referee facilitates the game by spotting and penalising destructive tactics and encouraging and rewarding constructive play. By doing so he creates the time and space necessary.

A useful checklist of management skills is as follows.

- Demonstration of an empathy for the game by letting it develop in accordance with the temper of the match.
- Management of verbal interactions with players so that it is evident that the referee is clear and confident.
- Identification and management of flash-points (e.g. bodies on the ground, problems at set-pieces, persistent offences).
- Avoidance of foul play originating from a lack of management in critical phases of play.
- Management of foul play and persistent infringement with appropriate action as required.
- Management of situations without resorting to penalties, except in situations where players do not respond.
- Demonstration of an intent to provide solutions to problems so that the same offences are not penalised throughout the match.
- Maintenance of concentration throughout the match.
- Confident decision making which is unaffected by the pace of the match, crowd or player pressure (especially when making difficult decisions which could have a major bearing on the outcome).

When a match is managed well, the referee clearly establishes credible relationships with the two teams. He sets clear priorities and is consistent in his application of the Laws. In keeping with his mandate, the good referee will always try to resolve problems early so that the match is not spoilt. It is important that the referee is consistent, firm and fair from the kick-off. Players want to know where they stand immediately, and it's the referee's duty to set those standards from the start and maintain them.

2 The basic principles

As an overriding priority, the referee has to abide by three fundamental principles: **Safety, Equity, and Laws**.

2.1 Safety

Rugby is a physically demanding sport. Quite apart from the obvious contact elements, there is now a much greater demand on fitness levels as the Laws have evolved to increase the speed and openness of the game. This combination may lead to situations where the referee will have to intervene to ensure the safety of the players involved.

It is therefore the referee's primary responsibility to ensure the safety of all players at all times. The players' safety takes precedence over everything else: **if it looks dangerous, stop it**. The good referee never compromises safety, and will be constantly alert to potential dangers - body positions in the tackle, scrum, line-out, ruck and maul - and use the whistle to prevent injury. A referee can always justify a decision to stop the progress of a match on the grounds of safety.

It cannot be stressed too often that the primary role of the referee is to protect the players. You cannot always protect them from themselves, if they are determined to place themselves in danger, but you must be there to make sure that they are protected from the consequences of their actions, however injudicious they may have been. Foul and dangerous play have no place in the game and, as the RFU says, the Laws provide all the necessary sanctions - as well as preventive measures - to allow a fair physical contest.

To attain this level of protection, the referee has numerous additional duties. The referee is not a policeman, nor is he the Law-maker. The referee is described in the Laws as the sole judge of fact and of Law; in other words, his decisions are final (with the proviso that he can change his decision based on information given to him by his touch judges). However, referees do not want to be seen solely as judges, nor do the players wish to treat them as such. Referring back to that earlier statement of the referee's objective, he is there to manage an environment in which both sides can play and enjoy the match within the Laws.

2.2 Equity

Players rightly assume that referees appointed to their games will be impartial, consistent and fair. This is the basic principle of equity. To apply this principle, referees need to demonstrate that they understand the game and have an empathy with the players and what they are trying to achieve. Applying the principle involves the following key elements of referee behaviour.

- He will be consistent, even-handed and fair.
- He will be firm, yet friendly and approachable.
- He will be positive and take control.
- He will set standards early and vigilantly maintain them.
- He will treat players sympathetically.
- He will play advantage to the full (other than for reasons of safety).
- He will take up positions which give him the best all-round view of the match.
- He will be polite, civil and expect the same standard from the participants.

This list seems daunting, especially when you consider some of the research on referees. On average, it has been estimated that a referee will make over 1,000 decisions during a match - a number that includes all those decisions not to blow the whistle. The referee will cover over four miles during a match, and 13% of that distance will be with backwards movement. Even during set pieces, referees are rarely still. As they are engaged in all this activity, they have to be thinking about the application of the Laws and the safety of the players. They also have to bear in mind that they must treat all 30 players the same, and that the players will have seen how the referee interprets their actions and what response he gives. Once a precedent is set, it must be followed, because that is what the players on both sides want and expect. This is part of the challenge the referee accepts and the reward is greater for a job well done.

2.3 Laws

Naturally, the referee must know and understand the Laws. The Law book is a start, but it is by no means the end. If you simply learn the Laws without ever bothering to understand the motives behind them, you will always have a problem managing your matches.

Many referees like to study a different Law every week; they will take each part of it and visualise situations in which its application will or might be relevant.

The skill of visualisation is something that will only come after a little experience with the whistle, but it is a skill that is well worth developing. It is vital that referees are able to translate the intentions of the Lawmakers into practical decision making. Good interpretation of the Laws is something that only comes with practice, and the good referee never stops learning.

3 Communication

However good you may be as a referee, your qualities count for nothing if you cannot communicate. You must let the players know what you expect, and explain your decisions clearly and succinctly.

Each referee develops his own style of communication, and it must be natural. You're there to let the players enjoy the game, and they want you to be decisive, firm yet approachable. Good referees develop a working relationship with the players. There are as many different ways of achieving this as there are referees, and you must be comfortable with your own. Listen to what other referees say, and watch how they communicate; study videos of the top matches, and go and watch your local side and see how the referee interacts. You will only know what's best for you once you're on the field, but you can learn some valuable lessons from others. Do not try and copy others, but adapt their better habits to suit yourself.

A cautionary note on communication: do not, under any circumstances, swear or use foul language. Remember also that communication is a two way process. If you talk to the players then they will talk to you. This chat should not necessarily be seen as a challenge, but rather an opportunity. A laugh on the pitch can smooth many problems.

Communicating with the players comes in three ways: **voice, whistle and body**.

3.1 The voice

The best referees talk to players all the time and prevent infringements. But players will always make mistakes, and some will try to overstep the boundaries in the hope that the referee doesn't spot them. This is the area where discretion plays such a vital role in the referee's skill set: spotting an infringement doesn't necessarily mandate whistling for it, especially if the non-infringing team gains an advantage. 'I saw what you did, Red 8, and don't do it again', is a very effective method of communicating without breaking up the flow of the game and denying advantage to the opposition.

Using clear oral communication is therefore vital to let players know what is and is not allowed in Law: 'Penalty kick to Red. Blue 2, you joined the maul in front of the hindmost player. You're offside.' One of the better acronyms to bear in mind is **ATP** - Advise, Tell, Penalise. Infringing players who are not interfering with play can be advised of what they're doing wrong, told once more if they repeat the offence, then penalised if they still haven't got the message. Obviously this doesn't apply to every situation, especially when foul play is involved, but it gets the message across without blowing for every infringement. Nobody wants to participate in a match where the referee blows for every incident, regardless of its bearing on the result. If players do not respond to being advised or told, they can *still* be penalised for that actual offence.

The voice can and should be used to prevent offences occurring, for example: 'Stay onside, 6. Release the ball. Roll away.' Players respond well to a referee who talks to them. The players don't want to have to guess what the referee is looking for, and what is or is not acceptable. If they have those parameters established for them, through clear and consistent instructions from the referee, they can concentrate on playing the game. In many games you'll find that the referee is almost constantly talking during the first 15 to 20 minutes, setting out his requirements straight away and managing the players so that they don't consistently infringe. But consistent chattering does not help the players if there is no purpose to it. Verbal communications must have a clear objective behind them: to prevent or to explain an infringement. Be brief, calm, specific.

The tone of voice used should be firm and positive, indicating that the referee is in control and will not accept any nonsense. The referee doesn't want to sound officious and out of touch, but needs to convey confidence and a sympathy with his players. Talk is always the preferred first option; the whistle should only be used when players choose not to listen. Don't be afraid to say 'please', 'thank you' or 'well done'.

3.2 The whistle

A whistle is remarkably versatile. Referee advisers will say that, when they are watching a good referee, they can stand with their backs to play and still know what the referee has blown for, so distinct are the different signals. A very loud and long blast will signify foul play; a loud blast for a penalty or a try; medium for the award of a scrum; and light for ball in touch or a conversion. The old adage of refereeing is: 'Think quick, blow slow.' The whistle should never be held in the mouth, but should be securely wrapped around the hand with a bootlace or with elastic.

3.3 The body

What about the body? The right body language is critical to the success of a referee. It includes how the referee is turned out: are the boots and kit clean, the hair neat, all the accoutrements (pencil, whistle, score-card, yellow/red cards, handkerchief) in good working order? Does he look fit to referee? It even extends beyond the pitch to the clubhouse: how does the referee look before and after the game? Does he arrive looking smart? Is he confident when he walks in before the match, and how does he look when he goes for a drink with the players after the game? We'll cover these aspects in more detail later in this chapter, the referee needs to create the right aura from the minute he arrives.

On the pitch, of course, the body plays a major part. The correct signals (*see* pp.105-15) need to be given clearly and crisply, so that all the players and spectators can see what is going on. Even if a referee is making all the right decisions, it is very frustrating if some of the players - or spectators - are unable to understand those decisions. Hand signals give the first indication of what the infringement was and against whom the decision is made. There is no room for customisation or flamboyance; as long as the signals are properly made, and visible to all interested parties, there should be nothing to complain about. Bear in mind that the size of a referee is important here: a tall referee has an advantage, and shorter ones need to ensure that their signals can be clearly seen, especially when they are surrounded by giant locks and flankers!

The general rule is that the visual signal will be the first indication by the referee of what has happened and what is going to happen: whistle; signal; explain. When there is a breakdown in open play, there may only be four or five players in earshot of the referee, so he needs to signal the reason for the stoppage before other players have arrived. Then he can say, for example: 'Knock on by Red 6. Scrum here. Blue ball.'

Time is at a premium, and yet the best referees seem to have a lot of it. They read the game so that they're always in the right position; they are never hurried, and always have the time to look around so that they are not solely concentrating on where the ball is. Whilst much of this comes from experience and fitness, and new referees cannot expect to do this from the start, players react positively to those referees who give the appearance of complete control. By being in the right place, and using a quick movement of the head to look back and see what's happening behind you, you win the players' respect. The backs don't know for sure if you've seen them creeping offside at a ruck, but an arm outstretched after one of these rapid glances can often achieve the desired effect, and they may not be tempted to try and gain an unfair advantage.

4 The team of three

Unfortunately, the role of the touch judge is much maligned and misunderstood. Far from being someone who is pulled from the bar to wave a grubby handkerchief from time to time, the touch judge is a vital assistant to the referee and can have a major influence on a match.

Law 6 states that: *There are two touch judges for every match. Unless they have been appointed by or under the authority of the match organiser, it shall be the responsibility of each team to provide a touch judge.* This is a part of the Laws which is rarely applied at the lower levels of the game, and junior referees tend to regard touch judges as something of a luxury. However, it is useful to learn about the management of touch judges and the way in which the team of three can work together to create a better match.

For the concept to work well, the referee has to brief the touch judges fully on what he wants and expects from them. Apart from the obvious priorities of marking touch and judging kicks at goal, tough judges appointed by a Society or the RFU can also help the referee to spot infringements in all the critical phases of play, and can mark out onside/offside lines for the players. There are recommended hand signals for foul play, offside, front row scrum offences and knock-ons, and the referee should know these signals. He can instruct the touch judges to perform a variety of duties, including keeping the score and the time and monitoring play in-goal, but he must not assume that his touch judges will know what he wants them to do. The pre-match briefing is therefore an important part of the referee's preparation.

Management of the team of three is in the hands of the referee, and his success is judged on the following criteria.

- Evidence of thorough briefing of touch judges.
- Foul play situations managed jointly.
- Evidence of communication and teamwork between the referee and touch judges.
- Referee supportive of touch judges.
- Demonstration of an ability to react to touch judge advisory signals.

Used effectively, touch judges add two pairs of eyes and ears to the management of the match and can draw the referee's attention to situations that might otherwise not be noticed and addressed. The referee remains the sole judge of fact and Law, but he can and should involve his touch judges to give him additional vision and coverage.

5 Preparation

Good preparation is vital to success. Referees invest significant time in activities separate from, but related to, the actual match. They train; they study; they teach others; they act as ambassadors; and they prepare for each appointment.

5.1 Advance planning

The Referee's Society will normally receive a monthly list of appointments, detailing the home side, the opposition, the time and the venue. This is when the referee starts his preparation: he needs to organise his transport, for instance, as well as thinking about the nature of each fixture. Is it a cup game, a friendly, a league match, an under-19 game? In the week before the fixture he will be contacted by the home club's fixtures secretary to confirm the details. This is the first opportunity the referee has to set his standards; in effect, the fixture starts with this call. The referee can and should ask about first aid facilities, touch judges (if none are appointed), the name of the captain, the precise location and phone number of the clubhouse, and the colours of both sides. If he needs to be picked up from the station, he should arrange it there and then. In this conversation he can convey his authority and his competence before he's even stepped on the pitch.

Once he has this information, the referee can start to plan. This will begin with his kit. All the kit needs to be clean and in good condition. The boots and their laces should be spotless. He will need three shirts - of completely different plain colours - and three pairs of shorts (white, black and navy blue) and socks. If he plans to warm up outside, he should have a track suit and trainers. It's easy to forget to pack a towel and toiletries; these are important because he needs to look as smart in the bar afterwards as he did when he arrived.

The referee carries an increasingly large number of accoutrements. Many referees have a special box in which they store it all (see list opposite).

If you belong to a Referee Society which uses grading cards for feedback from the clubs on referee performance, these should be filled out as much as possible before you leave home (and put a stamp on them), but bear in mind that, in more junior matches, the opposition sometimes turns out to be different to that expected, or you may be asked to cover a different fixture at the last minute.

- Two whistles (Acme Thunderers are recommended).
- Two sharpened, short pencils.
- Score-cards (with a waterproof holder so that they don't get sodden in the rain).
- Yellow and red cards.
- Stud measure, spare studs, and stud key.
- Clean handkerchief (useful for removing mud and dirt from players' eyes).
- Coin for the toss.
- Sock garters.
- Spare laces.
- Two watches (preferably with stop-watch and/or count-down facility).
- The Law book.

5.2 The right diet

Referees have lots of problems with their eating schedule before a match. When you run on the field, if your glycogen levels are low your capacity to maintain the necessary work rate for 80 minutes will be impaired, so how you have eaten during the days prior to the match will have an influence.

It's therefore desirable to have an adequate intake of carbohydrate in preparation for a match. In the week leading up to a match, and especially the last couple of days, there should be an increased carbohydrate intake. But this does not mean that you should stuff yourself! There should be a gradual increase in carbohydrate and fluid throughout the week. Take smaller, more frequent high carbohydrate meals which are easier on the stomach. Last minute stockpiling is harmful rather than helpful, so the meal on Friday evening should be relatively light.

Any meal on match day should ideally be taken a good 3 to 4 hours before kick-off to allow plenty of time for digestion. One important reason for this is that anxiety tends to slow down the rate at which food moves through the system. The meal should be light, easily digestible and consist mainly of carbohydrates. Fluid intake is obviously very important and must be maintained. Always take a source of food and drink in your bag for emergencies.

5.3 Match day procedure

As a general rule, the more senior the match, the earlier you should arrive at the ground. As a rule of thumb, you should arrive two hours before a RFU match and one hour before other level matches if possible. In any event, you need to plan an early arrival to give yourself plenty of time to get in the right physical and mental state, and to attend to some important pre-match issues. Look the part - a referee who arrives wearing a blazer, Society tie and smart trousers and shoes will immediately create a more favourable impression than one who turns up looking dishevelled and disorganised. Additionally, you'll be instantly recognisable as the referee if you're smartly dressed.

If an adviser has been assigned to your match he will introduce himself to you as early as possible and will then leave you be. He understands that this pre-match period is a busy time and that you have other concerns; remember that he's been through it himself. Do not worry about the presence of an adviser; as his title suggests, he's there to help you improve your game, not hurl criticism at you. If you have been given qualified touch judges, you must make contact with them early and give them clear instructions as to what you require from them.

At the lower levels both team captains may be struggling to find 15 players, and they will appreciate knowing that they have one less thing to worry about if they have a referee. Introduce yourself to the home captain; ask if they have a first aid box and stretcher, and find out if there is a qualified medical representative on site. You should also arrange a time to do the stud and dress check. Some teams like to go out and warm up before returning to the changing room for a final briefing, whilst others do not come back. Ask both skippers what their routine is, and tell them when you want to do the check - in the changing room is preferable to out on the field. You should also try to arrange the toss before they go out. It is usually best to arrange this as early as possible to allow you all to prepare.

At this stage you can also request touch judges but, especially with junior sides, be prepared that you will not have any. If that is the case, tell both captains that you are there to referee, not run touch, so that they understand your role and expectations. You should also confirm the kick-off time to avoid any misunderstanding. Be friendly but keep your discussion with the captains brief and to the point; they don't want to be bothered with you any more than is necessary.

If, as is often the case, there is no separate changing room for officials and you are asked to share with the home team, make sure you leave enough time to change before the team comes in. They need their privacy and they won't want you encroaching on it. If necessary, change immediately and go out; the players will appreciate your sensitivity.

Your first task outside is to inspect the pitch. Is it properly marked out? Are there overhanging trees or other obstructions? If there is more than one pitch, do the lines run parallel to each other or are there overlaps? How deep are the in-goal areas? Are they the same at both ends? Are all the required flags in place? Are there post protectors, and are the posts themselves secure? Where is the sun, and will it get in your eyes and affect your vision? As you inspect the pitch you should be walking off the journey and getting yourself attuned to the task ahead. This is often the time when referees feel most stress, and many like to have a set routine which deals with it. Develop your own schedule, but don't make it so hard and fast that, if anything changes, your confidence will be adversely affected.

5.4 Dealing with stress

Everyone copes with stress in a different way. As you become more experienced you will learn how to live with it more effectively, but it is perfectly healthy and normal to have some level of stress. It helps to think about what you are trying to achieve, and what your priorities should be. Some referees can visualise situations that may occur during a match and how they will handle them. The major priorities will always run along similar lines.

- **General** - to prevent flash-points in which players become involved in foul play.
- **Open play** - to keep players on their feet and onside.
- **Scrum** - to keep the scrum up, both for safety reasons and to get the ball back into play as quickly and cleanly as possible.
- **Line-out** - to concentrate on offences across the line-out, because they tend to be destructive.
- **Rucks and mauls** - to keep players on their feet and to restrict infringements, i.e. straying offside.

Concentrating on these basic priorities will help you to prepare psychologically. There are also useful relaxation techniques to assist in dealing with anxiety. When nervous or apprehensive, there is a tendency to breathe quickly and not deeply enough. The part of the breathing process that is frequently performed incorrectly is exhaling. In order to acquire the optimum amount of oxygen for the system to stimulate awareness and brain functions, the following exercises are recommended.

1 This exercise can be used at any time prior to kick-off to ensure that the anxiety level is at the optimal level.

• Breathe out quite strongly to exhale all the stale air from the lungs.
• Breathe in and hold the breath for a count of eight.
• Let the air exhale gently.
• Wait for a count of five and see if your finger-tips tingle slightly, which indicates that oxygen is circulating well in the blood stream. At this point you should begin to feel relaxed yet alert.

2 This exercise is longer term and will generate deep relaxation, so it is not useful immediately before a game but very good in the days preceding a match or on the morning of the match.

• Close your eyes and focus the mind on your toes and be aware of how they feel. Tense the feet slightly and then release the tension.
• Carry out the same procedure with calves, thighs and stomach, working up through the body to include the face and scalp.
• Finish by focussing on your breathing and noticing that it is slow and even. When you are ready, open your eyes and experience the feeling of calm and well-being which results from this exercise.

5.5 Final preparation

When you are back in the changing room, check your kit again and lay out everything you will need to take with you. If you know that you will have to travel some distance to the pitch, be sure to pack your spares to take with you - no-one wants the match held up while you race back to the changing room for a new pencil.

Once you are changed, check again on the two teams to see if they are going to have full sides; you should be especially concerned about the front rows, as you will need to play uncontested scrums if either side cannot raise a qualified front row.

At this stage you should go through your own physical routine, stretching and exercising to get the muscles warm and ready for action. Your warm-up needs to be fairly close to kick-off time so that you don't lose the benefits.

An effective warm-up.

1 Gentle jog for 3-5 minutes (including jogging backwards and sideways).
2 High knee raises for 15-20 metres, walk back and repeat four times. Bring the knees up higher than parallel to the ground; pick up speed of movement; try to maintain the knee lift; don't tense up; stay relaxed.
3 Flicks for 15-20 metres, walk back and repeat four times. Flick heels up quickly to seat; leave your hands by your side and allow feet to tap hands each time; keep body upright.
4 Sprint for 20 metres, walk back and repeat five times. Start by striding out at approximately three-quarters pace and progressively increase pace with each sprint.

The warm-up should also include some stretching, either after or in between the suggested activities. It is equally advisable to warm down after a training session or game to help the adaptations which the body has to bring about in the recovery phase. This can be done with mild, rhythmic muscular activity, such as jogging or skipping, which gradually decreases in intensity. Stretching is also recommended.

Your final action before going out to the pitch should be the stud and dress check. The Laws are very precise about what is, and what is not, allowed, and you must adhere to these strictures for the players' safety. Some referees do a roaring trade in selling legal studs to players before the game! If you have the resources, carry spare studs with you so that you can help the players.

With regard to dress, there is a fine line to be drawn. Referees are not expect-ed to frisk every player and check their hands for rings, and you must put the onus on the players to show you if they think they're wearing something that might be illegal. Warn them of the consequences if they do not do this; Law 4 (Players' Clothing) authorises the referee to send off a player who is wearing an illegal item.

Law 6 (Match Officials) forbids the referee from giving *any advice to either team prior to the match*. However, you must exercise a degree of discretion about this. Whilst you have all the players together in the changing room you have your first opportunity to tell them of your expectations. Be brief, firm and friendly by reminding them to stay on their feet, and onside, you are taking pre-ventive measures - if they don't comply during the match, they have only themselves to blame. Additionally, telling the front rows how you will set the scrum could avoid problems later on. Be aware that many players have never seen a Law book, so if they ask questions, especially at the beginning of the season when there may be new Law changes, try to be helpful without compromising yourself. There's another good reason for talking to the players before the match: it gets them used to your voice, which they'll be hearing a lot on the pitch. If you have touch judges, make sure they talk to the players as well - they, too, will be communicating during the game and the players need to know how they sound. Finally, whatever you have said, remember to wish them good luck and a good match.

Expect the sides to be out on time and ready for the kick-off as scheduled, but exercise a degree of tolerance in junior matches where the sides may be still be struggling to raise a full 15. It's much better to wait five minutes for a prop to arrive than to kick off without him.

6 After the match

You will experience the full gamut of emotions after a match. When you have finished your first one, the major feeling will be one of enormous relief that it's all over. As you get more experience you become more critical, and you tend to focus on the things that did not go as well as you'd hoped. There may have been particular incidents which unsettled you - a sending off, a disallowed try, a collapsed scrum, a bad injury - or an area of the Laws which you didn't manage very effectively. As you warm down, or pull off your boots, thoughts of these will undoubtedly dominate. Very few referees come back to the changing room with the feeling that they have achieved everything they'd planned. That's human nature, and it's hard to fight against it. After all, you will only improve your skills if you are constructively critical of your own performance.

You may have little time for quiet reflection, especially if you're sharing a changing room with one of the teams. The players will be talking about the match, and some of their remarks may be designed to wind you up. Keep your counsel: an unguarded response to some criticism from a player may be very damaging, not just for you but for every referee who subsequently comes to the club. Don't loiter in the changing room; take your shower early and let the players relax and unwind without you inhibiting their discussion. It is, however, very important that you make yourself available to all the players after the match. There are two main reasons for this.

Firstly, you can help the players by discussing their concerns and improving their understanding of the Laws. Very often they will want clarification of a point of Law - when does a line-out end, for example? - and you should discuss

THE PRINCIPLES OF MANAGEMENT

this with them without getting into the details of every decision you made. You will also learn much from this discussion: you'll find out how they interpret the Laws, and possibly how other referees have approached similar issues (although you must never comment on another referee's performance). The decisions you make on the pitch are final, and that's that; don't let yourself get compromised by too much debate on specific issues related to the match. Don't be afraid to admit to mistakes: the players know you're only human, and you'll be much better regarded if you demonstrate this! Secondly, remember that rugby is still predominantly a social sport, played for pleasure rather than gain. The after-match drinks in the bar are usually friendly and fun, and the referee, as part of the game, should participate - even if he only drinks orange juice and lemonade! You do not want the players to think that you're unapproachable and superior - either on or off the pitch.

If you have been watched by an adviser, he will be waiting for you in the club bar. He'll be sympathetic about you needing to mix with the players, and he'll try and fit in his session with you around that. He'll find a quiet corner for you both to go through his assessment of your performance, and to discuss any problems or questions you may have. Don't waste the opportunity to talk with an adviser - he can offer an enormous amount of practical advice as to what he thought went well as well as problems.

You must make sure that you thank both captains for the match and, where appropriate, anyone from the club who ran the line or helped you in other ways. If the match was a competitive fixture you will probably be asked to sign team sheets and confirm the score.

7 Fit to referee

Fitness is not an absolute state. It is relative, and comes in many different forms. The rugby player requires different fitness attributes to, say, a squash player or a boxer. The pace of rugby union has changed so dramatically over the last decade that there are no longer any hiding places for the unfit; the game has developed to such an extent that today's top forwards are almost as quick and mobile as backs were ten years ago. Progressive Law changes have succeeded in making a faster game with rapid recycling of the ball and fewer stoppages. The demands of competitive, open rugby - in league and international fixtures - have highlighted the need for much higher levels of fitness.

As the 31st player on the pitch, the referee's fitness has also assumed much more importance. With so much at stake in competitive matches, the responsibility of the referee to keep up with play has greatly increased. It is no longer acceptable to make judgements some 15 or 20 metres from the ball. Whilst fit-ness alone cannot guarantee a better standard of refereeing, it certainly allows the referee a better opportunity of being in the best position to make correct decisions. Those who have come to refereeing because they could no longer maintain their fitness level for playing are in for a rude shock! (There is more information on the whole subject of fitness and diet in the RFU's booklet, 'Fit to Referee and Touch Judge'.)

7.1 The basics of fitness

For the purposes of the rugby referee, fitness can be broken down into six dif-ferent elements.

- **Aerobic endurance** is the capacity of a referee to maintain continuous activity over a long period of time.
- **Muscular endurance** represents the capacity for continuous performance of relatively localised muscular activity.
- **Strength** is the capacity to exert a force against a resistance, ranging from explosive, powerful movements to more statically applied strength.
- **Speed** is the ability to run fast, to accelerate, to change direction and react quickly.
- **Flexibility** is the freedom to move the body through a wide range of motions and positions.
- **Agility** involves speed of movement, and a change of direction, in a controlled, balanced way.

Before getting into the detail of how to achieve and maintain these compo-nents, we should consider the basics of fitness. One important principle of physiological fitness is that the major body systems - in particular the heart, lungs and circulation (known as the cardio-vascular system) - benefit from being challenged. This system is very trainable and it thrives from operating at higher levels. This is what separates humans from machines: the body can adapt and improve its efficiency as a result of work.

The basis to fitness training is endurance, which ensures that the muscles can call on enough energy to enable them to keep working and delay the onset of fatigue. The two vital factors in the provision of energy are **oxygen supply** and **nutrition**.

Oxygen is brought into the body by the lungs, and transported in the blood, which is pumped round the body by the heart. Energy is supplied in the body by several systems. One of these is the aerobic system, in which energy is produced in the presence of oxygen (aerobic means with oxygen). This energy system is important for continuous work, for keeping going for 80 minutes. It is a long term energy supply. But the aerobic system often fails to meet the needs of referees during the game, especially when they have to perform several hard sprints with only brief periods of rest. Although the aerobic system is a vital and efficient energy system, it is often unable to supply energy at a sufficiently high rate, such as in a sprint, so additional energy is supplied by the anaerobic systems.

One of these anaerobic systems, glycolysis, uses glycogen stored in the muscle to deliver rapid energy and, over a short period of time, this system can supply enough energy to cope with very intensive work. The problem is that lactic acid is also released which is a cause of fatigue in the body, and eventually the need to slow down or stop becomes apparent. With the right kind of training - e.g. shuttle running - the body's tolerance to lactic acid can be raised.

Referees can also improve their fitness through strength work. Although referees do not need the same high levels of strength and power as players, they should work on appropriate strength training programmes to develop qualities such as muscular endurance and acceleration.

There is another aspect to physical fitness: *Mens sana in corpore sano* (A healthy mind in a healthy body). If you are physically fit, your mental faculties are much sharper. When you arrive at a break-down in open play, and a ruck or maul develops, you need to be alert to all the potential infringements. If you're unfit, you'll find yourself struggling to make those decisions: you'll be too tired, and too concerned with your own recovery, to give your full attention to the game. But if you're in good physical condition, you'll have one less thing to worry about.

7.2 Principles of training

You cannot hope to get and stay fit simply by refereeing on a Saturday afternoon; you can, however, train the body and energy systems in advance so that the 80 minutes you spend on the pitch are as pleasant and enjoyable as possible. To achieve any increase in fitness, the referee has to train a little harder - the principle of overload. For training to have any impact, it must overload the system sensibly. When that happens, the body adapts to the load, so that what was once exceptional becomes standard. Subtle changes in the body take place as it adapts to the added demands imposed on it; but the body adapts slowly and any attempt to rush the process may well result in injury, illness or both.

The principle of adaptation works by making demands where intensity and duration force the body to adjust its performance upwards. This increases the body's tolerance for more activity of even greater intensity. The improvement is not a straight line on a graph: individuals have different tolerances, and the degree of intensity or severity of the exercise must be varied accordingly as the training progresses.

This progression needs a careful and sensible build-up of training over weeks and months, stage by stage. If the training loads are increased too quickly the body will not be able to adapt. On the other side of the coin, there is the problem of reversibility. Any improvement in fitness is purely temporary. Fitness is hard to gain and easy to lose, so it's important to maintain fitness work on a regular basis.

Finally, the fitness regime needs to be varied. If the same exercises are carried out day after day then boredom and staleness will soon set in. Variation of exercise and training regimes will maintain motivation and interest. It also helps to train with someone else - many referees work with their local rugby club.

7.3 Fitness programmes

As we've already noted, fitness is subjective and has to be built around the demands and needs of the individual, so it is inappropriate to set out lists of training schedules. There are, however, some basic principles that apply to all referees.

- Start your endurance training during the summer, aiming for four sessions a week - you must be fit when the season starts or you'll never catch up.
- Develop a programme that is appropriate - take advice from professionals.
- By the start of the season you should be doing two endurance sessions and one speed session in addition to your matches.
- Remember that speed is just as vital as stamina - you must work on your sprinting.
- Swimming, squash, tennis, etc. are all good forms of exercise which are also enjoyable - use them as part of your programme.
- Don't overdo it at first - build up sensibly. As we get older the body takes more time to adapt, and more time to recover.
- Vary the weekly routine to maintain your interest and to develop different fitness attributes.
- Don't forget warm-up/warm-down sessions - many injuries occur because these are not properly carried out.

7.4 Nutrition and diet

You may have heard of the acronym GIGO - 'Garbage In, Garbage Out'. This applies to diet: if you eat badly then your body will respond accordingly. Whilst no-one wishes to be a slave to refereeing, there are some sensible guidelines for eating that will enhance performance and help your body to recover between exercise sessions.

We know that improvements in fitness are the result of the body adapting to the stresses of training. This adaptation requires that the body takes in all the necessary nutrients, so you must pay attention to your eating habits 365 days of the year - not just on those few days prior to matches. To ensure that your diet meets the demands placed on your body, you should consume sufficient energy in the form of **carbohydrates** so that you can maintain the stores of energy within the muscles.

Carbohydrates are stored within the muscle in the form of glycogen. As mentioned earlier, glycogen is released by the muscles to deliver rapid energy when there is an oxygen deficit. You can only replace it by eating or drinking substances that contain carbohydrates. The emphasis should be on complex carbohydrates: bread, potatoes, rice, pasta, pulses, cereals, vegetables (especially root vegetables and green leafy vegetables), fresh fruit (apples, bananas, oranges) and dried fruit (apricots, prunes).

Try to reduce the overall amount of fat in your diet. Start off by decreasing consumption of all visible fat (butter, lard, oils, meat fat) and non-visible fat (milk, dairy produce, eggs, mayonnaise, sausages, pâté, pies and pastry). In contrast to carbohydrates, fat cannot be used as an immediate energy supply.

Finally, ensure that you maintain a high fluid intake by drinking plenty of water and fresh fruit juice as part of your normal diet.

8 Foul play

Foul play is, happily, a rare occurrence in the game of rugby union, largely because coaches and referees have worked very hard to convince players that it is unacceptable; additionally, the disciplinary committees have wide discretion to impose hefty suspensions on players who are found guilty of foul play.

Every referee will have to deal with a foul play situation and it needs to be handled with equal measures of firmness, diplomacy and pragmatism. You should always bear in mind, with this Law as with all others, that the onus on compliance lies with the players - especially the captains - and the coaches. The Laws clearly set out the parameters, and you are there to see that the game is conducted within those parameters, but you must not take sole responsibility for ensuring that the game is played in a sporting spirit. Captains also carry a heavy responsibility for the discipline of their sides, as do the coaches, and you will occasionally need to remind them of that.

8.1 The authority of the referee

Before getting into the details of foul play and how to handle it, there is one other Law which is particularly relevant: Law 6, Referee and Touch Judges. Law 6 is important because it lays down some unequivocal statements about the referee's authority. For example: *The referee is the sole judge of fact and of Law. All players must respect the authority of the referee. They must not dispute the referee's decisions.* Offences by players under Law 6 are to be treated as misconduct, and dealt with under the provisions of Law 10. This means that dissent is normally penalised with a penalty kick; however, if the dissent follows the award of a penalty kick, the referee has the power to advance the mark of the kick a further 10 metres. If the original penalty was a free kick, the referee can change this to a penalty kick as a result of dissent from the offending team. He can also reverse a decision if there is dissent. Law 6 therefore establishes the authority of the referee, but do not confuse this with respect: that has to be earnt from the players by displaying safety, equity and law knowledge, and application.

8.2 Foul play infringements

Basically, actions of foul play can be divided into two categories - those that endanger the safety of other players, and those that are contrary to the Laws and spirit of the game.

8.2.1 Dangerous play and misconduct

Remembering the referee's primary duty to ensure the safety of all the players, dangerous play must be severely penalised. Dangerous play includes the following.

- Early and late tackles.
- Striking, hacking, kicking, tripping or trampling on an opponent.
- Charging or obstructing an opponent who has just kicked the ball.
- Holding, pushing, charging, obstructing or grasping an opponent not holding the ball (except in a scrummage, ruck or maul).
- Forming the scrummage some distance from the opponents and rushing against them on engagement.
- Lifting opponents in the front row of a scrummage.
- Collapsing a scrummage, ruck or maul.

Guidance to referees is unequivocal: *A player guilty of dangerous play shall either be ordered off or else cautioned that he will be ordered off if he repeats the offence.* There certainly appears to be no room for doubt here, and yet the referee has to make critical decisions - with help from his touch judges, if present - on what constitutes dangerous play and what is merely accidental or clumsy. Some of the Law's definitions of dangerous play include the word 'wilfully': this suggests that the referee needs to interpret the intention of the player when deciding on the nature of the infringement. For instance, a ruck forms in which there are bodies on the ground, and a player joins the ruck and, in attempting to get his boot on the ball, rakes a grounded player with his studs. Is it intentional or accidental? Only the referee can decide and, in reaching that decision, much weight must be given to the temper of the match.

There should, however, be no differentiation between wilful and reckless behaviour. If a player acts in a reckless way, so that his action is likely to endanger others, he should be punished without regard for intent. Dangerous play, however initiated and for whatever reason, must be dealt with strictly.

The best advice is obviously to prevent potential flash-points. Experienced referees exercise their judgement on the temper of the match and manage it accordingly. If, for example, the match clearly has the potential for foul play - a local derby, a critical cup battle or a vital league match - the referee is likely to be particularly firm so that the players understand that dangerous play will not be tolerated. Cautions are one method of controlling the behaviour of players, as they send a message to all the players that the referee is in charge and will not allow dangerous play to go unpunished. Referees who do not adhere to this policy are doing a disservice to all the players, coaches, spectators and other referees.

8.2.2 Other foul play

There are three other actions which constitute foul play: obstruction, unfair play and repeated infringements.

Obstruction basically occurs when one player, who is not carrying the ball, interferes with another illegally.

This includes:
- charging or pushing an opponent running for the ball (except shoulder to shoulder)
- being in an offside position (i.e. in front of the ball) and running or standing in front of a team-mate carrying the ball, thus shielding him from opponents
- taking the ball from a scrum, ruck, maul or line-out and running back into his own players
- as a back-row player, changing body position at a scrummage to prevent an opponent moving round the scrummage.

All these infringements result in a penalty kick (or a penalty try).

Unfair play is unsportsmanlike conduct, and includes the following.

- Deliberately playing unfairly, or wilfully infringing any Law of the game (penalty kick).
- Wilfully wasting time (free kick).
- Wilfully knocking or throwing the ball from the playing area into touch, touch-in-goal or over the dead-ball line (free kick).

Repeated infringement is self-explanatory, and results in a penalty kick and, if necessary, a caution and subsequent dismissal.

8.3 Dealing with foul play

Law 10 gives a very broad definition: *Foul Play is anything a person does within the playing enclosure that is against the letter and spirit of the Laws of the Game. It includes obstruction, unfair play, dangerous play, repeated infringement and misconduct.* These actions nearly always result in a penalty kick, or penalty try, in favour of the non-infringing team. However, Law 10 also gives the referee the power to caution players for offences committed under this Law, and to order them off.

Some people say that a referee has somehow failed in his duty if he needs to resort to cautions and dismissals. This is completely wrong: it is one of the referee's primary duties to ensure that players guilty of foul play are severely punished, and that their actions are not seen to be condoned. You cannot allow a match to continue with players who are determined to breach the letter and spirit of the game, as this ruins it for all the other players and may well lead to further problems as players decide to take the Law into their own hands.

When you have decided to caution or dismiss a player, the one important principle to remember is that you must stay in control. If you lose your temper, using bad language or violent gestures, you run the risk of further inflaming the situation and losing the respect of the players. Take your time: take the offending player(s) away from the others, walking backwards if necessary so that you can continue to watch what is going on. The captain(s) should come with you - it can help if he knows what is going on and what you're proposing to do. Make your point succinctly: 'You pushed a player illegally; if you use foul play again you'll be ordered from the field of play'; explain the offence. Do not shout. Remember you are not the guilty one. Make your decision and the reasons for it absolutely clear to the player(s) and the captain(s). You must show the player either a yellow or red card, but you are not expected to brandish it flamboyantly! The cards are a confirmation of your decision, and are not to be used to abrogate your responsibility to communicate.

You must note down a number of details in addition to the player's full name, team, position and number. You have to record the score at the time, the time of the offence, the half in which it took place, the distance you were from the incident and whether you had a clear or obstructed view of it. All these details are needed for the Disciplinary Body.

A further point here concerns the option of a general team warning. Law 10 authorises the referee to give a general warning after repeated infringements, but it also gives the referee the discretion to decide whether a series of offences by different players of the same team amounts to repeated infringement. If the referee decides that it does, then he can issue a general warning to the team and, if the offence is repeated, he must order the offending player from the field. It could be unfair, punishing a player who has done nothing wrong for the rest of the game. Caution players one by one and, if necessary, send them off. If there is persistent infringement, warn the captain that the next player will get a caution and the following player after that will be ordered from the field of play.

Of course, there will be times when you choose not to caution or dismiss a player but you still want to give him an admonishment. Follow the same procedures as above, taking him away from the other players before telling him why you are talking to him. A few well-chosen words of sensible advice can often prevent worse incidents occurring later in the game. Do not hesitate to take both captains to one side if you feel the players are not responding positively to you and your decisions: put the onus on them to get their players to conform with the Laws and respect your decisions and authority.

When you have touch judges appointed under Law 6, use them and look out for their signals on foul play. Consult them and, when they have signalled for foul play, ask them for all the necessary details and their recommendation for the penalty.

There is one aspect of foul play that perturbs referees, and that is the brawl. The first rule is not to get between the brawling players: nobody expects you to sort out two or more props having a go at each other! Blow your whistle loudly once and again until order is restored. Take your time to separate and speak to the offenders and the captains. Time is essential to help calm everybody down. Segregate the two teams and speak to the captains.

8.4 Foul play - referee's checklist

When referees manage foul play effectively, the following elements are observed.

- Potential flash-points (e.g. pile-ups, collapsed scrums) are quickly dealt with.
- The game is managed in accordance with its temper.
- Touch judges are used effectively as extra pairs of eyes and ears.
- Referee's positioning allows him to see all aspects of the game, both on and off the ball.
- Offenders are swiftly and effectively penalised.

9 Understanding the game

Referees are an integral part of the game of rugby. They are active and vital participants, and they are vested with significant authority and influence. Their decisions on the pitch, and their behaviour off it, both contribute to the general health of the game.

You are there to help the players, to manage the game with due regard to equity, safety and the Laws. As a consequence, the good referee makes every effort to understand the game fully at all levels.

The obvious place to start is at the club. The vast majority of referees are already club members, and have played the game at some level. The link between a referee and his club is a vital, but often under-utilised, channel of communication. You will probably know many of the players already, as well as the coaches and officials, so spend time with them and find out what they're thinking about the game, and how they play it. Join them for pre-season training, and watch the set-piece manoeuvres; offer your advice to the coaches, so that they know how referees are likely to interpret different situations. They may not want or accept your advice, but most are very happy to hear another informed point of view.

You can also get involved with mini- and youth rugby, where clubs are always keen to take on new coaches; if the senior players of the future are taught how to play the game within the Laws, you'll be doing an enormous service. Additionally, you should be another medium of communication for mid-season changes in Law or interpretation. Although clubs are always advised of such changes, the information doesn't always filter down to players and coaches as quickly as it should, and you can ensure that they do know what's happening - and why.

If you find yourself without a fixture on a Saturday afternoon, go and watch a match - or, better still, offer to run the line. You'll find that you have a completely different perspective as a referee. Many referees say that they have to record matches on television so that they can watch them twice: once to see what the referee does and once to enjoy the match. You will naturally find yourself watching the referee, and you should learn from what he does. But you should also take the opportunity to study the players and how they behave. When you're refereeing, there are many times when you come off at the end of a match and you have no idea of what kind of game it was and what the overall strategy of each team was. You've been so focussed on the micro-view that you haven't had a chance to appreciate the larger picture. Watching from the sidelines helps to develop that vision, and gives you a better understanding. And don't confine yourself to watching senior rugby. Go out on a Sunday morning and you'll find some very high quality colts fixtures played to the under-19 Law variations.

There are many other ways to enhance your perspective of the game. We all know that the media has a completely different view of rugby, and that they tend to be interested only in the big matches. Read the press reports of these games, and see if the referee is mentioned: if he isn't, it probably means he had a very good game! Watch rugby programmes on television and see how the commentators and summarisers deal with different issues: do they know and understand the Laws? In some cases they don't, but it's useful to hear what others think of referees and their decisions. As importantly, their analysis of coaching strategies and tactics can teach you a lot about how the game is being played, and what you should be looking out for.

CHAPTER 3

Continuity

Everyone enjoys a rugby match which flows well and where the ball is constantly recycled quickly and brought back into open play. Referees have a major part to play in facilitating this, and the way in which they manage situations undoubtedly has a significant influence on how the game develops.

Continuity is all about setting the right platform so that the ball continues to move and does not become static or trapped. Although it is primarily the responsibility of the players to achieve good continuity, the referee can help by using preventive and punitive measures.

The phases of play which fall under this heading are **Law 15 - tackle, ball-carrier brought to the ground; ruck and maul; advantage; and open play.**

1 Law 15 - tackle, ball-carrier brought to the ground

Although Law 15 is a relatively short one, it is also very complex. Because of this, it is vital that the referee is always up with play and arrives at the break-down quickly so that he can see exactly what is happening and can give preventive instructions to the players. Effective management of Law 15 is absolutely critical to ensuring continuity in the game: when it is refereed well there will be a free-flowing match; when it is not, the match becomes static.

Essentially, therefore, Law 15 deals with situations where the ball-carrier or the ball goes to ground, and the major underlying principle of the Law is that players can only participate if they are on their feet. Once they have gone to ground, they must take positive action to get up before they can play the ball or tackle other players.

1.1 The tackle

According to the Law: ... *a tackle occurs when a ball-carrier is simultaneously held by one or more opponents and is brought to the ground and/or the ball touches the ground*. A player is not tackled if he is merely held and stays on his feet without releasing the ball.

There are three primary areas of focus for the referee at the point of tackle: the tackler(s), the tackled player and the arriving player(s).

The **tackler** is under an obligation to do something positive if he goes to ground in the making of the tackle. He must release the tackled player and get up or move away from the tackled player and the ball, and **he cannot play the ball until he is on his feet again**. When the tackler is on his feet he can attempt to play the ball; the tackled player must release the ball. If he gets in the way of opponents, interferes with play whilst on the ground, or prevents opponents from getting to the ball, he must be penalised. When the tackler moves out of the way, he enables the tackled player to comply with the Laws; the referee can help in this process by telling the tackler to 'Move away'. Strict refereeing of the tackler is vital for a quick free flowing game.

In addition to these restrictions, referees should also pay attention to Law 10, Foul Play. Early, late and dangerous tackles - including the stiff-arm tackle and tackles above the line of the shoulders - are very serious infringements, and the referee is advised: *Players who wilfully resort to this type of foul play must be ordered from the field*. Similarly, a player who charges or knocks down the ball-carrier without any effort to grasp or hold him, or who tackles a player who is off the ground when fielding a kick, is guilty of dangerous play and must be punished severely.

The **tackled player** has a number of options, which can be learnt by use of the acronym **PORAGOM**.

He must immediately ...

Pass the ball
Or
Release the ball
And
Get up
Or
Move away from the ball.

If there is one word in the Laws which causes more problems of interpretation than any other, it must surely be 'immediately'. Some referees work on the basis that the word contains five syllables and that the tackled player's action should take no longer than it takes to say the word. However, there are shades of interpretation that are dependent upon the circumstances. For instance, if the last man in defence is tackled near to his goal-line and has no support, and the tackler gets to his feet straight away, the ball release must be rapid. If, however, he is in midfield and is well supported, he may take slightly longer to place the ball as long as there is no unreasonable delay and his side are clearly in control.

Even if he releases the ball immediately, the tackled player must not simply lie on the ground and assume that there is no more to be done. He must make an effort to roll away or get up, unless it would be more dangerous to do this than to stay on the deck. The referee should encourage him by shouting 'Move away!'. If he doesn't, and the referee thinks he could have, he must be penalised.

There are many situations which look inherently illegal but are, in fact, perfectly permissible. Law 15 allows the tackled player to release the ball, or place it, or push it along the ground, in any direction as long as it is not forward and the action is immediate. This includes the situation where a tackled player falls so that he is facing the opposition goal-line; he is entitled to bring the ball over his body and push or throw it sideways or backwards towards his own goal-line. It looks terrible, but it's legal! What he is not allowed to do is roll over the ball so that he is then facing his goal-line.

The tackled player can also score a try, or make a touch-down on or behind his own goal-line, if he complies with the Laws: again, the emphasis here is on the immediacy of his action. If a tackled player's momentum carries the player into the in-goal, the player can score a try or make a touch down. Also, if players are tackled near to the goal line, these players may immediately reach out and ground the ball on or over the goal line to score a try or make a touch down.

At the tackle, **arriving players** must also comply with the basic principle of staying on their feet. These players must not go to ground and can only play the ball when they are on their feet. The only exception to this is when, following a tackle, the ball travels into the in-goal area: a player may then fall on the ball for a try or touch-down. The body position of arriving players will give the referee a good indication as to their intentions. Ideally, the players should be in a crouched position with straight backs and heads looking up. If they are rushing in with bent backs and heads down then they are likely to fall over, and can be penalised as they are making no effort to stay on their feet.

The referee can effectively manage the tackle situation with good communication. When the tackled player goes to ground and is still holding the ball, the referee should shout 'Release!'. Both the tackled player and the tackler need to be reminded of their duty to move away - 'Get away!' - and the arriving players must be encouraged to conform with the Laws - 'Stay on your feet!'. Remember, too, that there is no offside in the tackle; as well as being good play, it is legal for the tackler to turn his opponent so that he is facing the wrong way. However, arriving players must also enter the tackle zone from behind the ball.

1.2 Law 14 - ball on the ground, no tackle

There are obviously circumstances in which a player who has not been tackled goes to ground in open play, the most obvious being when he is covering an opponent's kick ahead. Again, this player is under an obligation to do something positive, and the same acronym **PORAGOM** can be used as a reminder.

The player going to ground must immediately get up on his feet with the ball or ...

Pass the ball *Or*
Release the ball *And*
Get up *Or*
Move away.

A player is not allowed to fall on or over the ball emerging from a scrum or ruck (unless the ball is in the in-goal area).

They must remain on their feet and not dive on the grounded player. It is imperative that arriving players must not voluntarily fall on or over players lying on the ground with the ball between them or near them - a shout of 'Stay up!' is a good reminder for these players.

1.3 Laws 14 and 15 - referee's checklist

As mentioned, the referee's primary concern is to ensure that the game is played only by those players on their feet. When the ball or a player goes to ground, the referee has to manage the situation firmly and quickly: when he does not, there are likely to be pile-ups of bodies and unproductive, static ball.

Under Laws 14 and 15, the referee will therefore:

- arrive at breakdowns quickly, and get into a position to manage the situation
- ensure that tacklers are not allowed to interfere with the release of the ball
- ensure that tackled players release and/or play the ball immediately
- keep arriving players on their feet
- prevent pile-ups, where bodies are on the ground and the ball is trapped, thus resulting in static play
- take preventive and punitive action.

2 Ruck and maul

One of the major challenges for referees is to identify and manage rucks and mauls. Well-managed rucks and mauls result in an exciting game, whilst badly-managed ones create static rugby and offer significant opportunities for flash-points and dangerous play. Perhaps the biggest challenge for the referee in these situations is knowing where the ball is, and that can only be achieved by good positioning. Along with this, the referee has to remember what happened immediately prior to the ruck or maul forming because, if the ball subsequently becomes unplayable, this will affect the decision on which side gets the put-in at the resulting scrum. Helpfully, the Laws give the referee guidance on this decision in those cases where he could not determine precisely who had control.

2.1 Ruck

Law 16 defines a ruck as follows. *A ruck is a phase of play where the ball is on the ground and one or more players from each team who are on their feet, in physical contact, close around the ball on the ground.*

This Law encourages the player in possession to get the ball on the deck and form a ruck as, if the ball subsequently becomes unplayable, the team moving forward prior to the stoppage will normally get the put-in at the resulting scrum. This contrasts with the maul Law, which awards the scrum the other way when the ball becomes unplayable.

Typically rucks are formed after a tackle or when a player has gone to ground to recover a loose ball. Remember that, according to the definition, players on the ground do not qualify as participants in a ruck: therefore, if the ball, the tackler and the tackled player are on the ground with no-one else there, it is not a ruck. Rucks can also be formed from mauls, where the ball is legally brought to the ground (as opposed to collapsing the maul, which is illegal).

Players advancing to the grounded ball should be permitted to take one step over the ball and any players lying near it. However, the practice known as 'scatter rucking', where players fan out and engage with opponents some distance from the ball, is illegal. Although handling in the ruck is not permitted - and is a penalty offence - it is acceptable for a player, such as the scrum-half, to recover the ball with his hands from the back of a ruck when it is obvious that his side has won control.

2.2 Maul

According to the Laws: *A maul occurs when a player carrying the ball is held by one or more opponents, and one or more of the ball carrier's team-mates on the ball carrier. All the players are on their feet.* This means that there must be **at least two players** from the side in possession of the ball **and an opponent** to constitute a maul. If the ball carrier is the only player from that team to be involved, opponents can come in from any direction to try and win the ball. N.B. This could be a flash point as players may think the joining players are offside! Use communication skills to confirm when a maul has been formed.

Coaches, players and referees all want the same things from a maul: they want it to be tidy and dynamic. When the maul is untidy - players wrestling for the ball, the maul lurching around or becoming static - there is little strategic advantage to be gained for either side, but most especially for the side in possession immediately prior to the start of the maul. When the ball in the maul becomes unplayable and it remains stationary or has stopped moving forward for longer than 5 seconds and a scrum is ordered, the ball is thrown in by the team not in possession when the maul began - so it makes sense for the side in possession to get the ball on the deck and create a ruck, to get the ball out of the maul as quickly as possible, or to keep the maul moving.

When a maul has stopped moving forward for more than 5 seconds but the ball is being moved and the referee can see it, a reasonable time is allowed for the ball to emerge. If it does not emerge within a reasonable time a scrum is ordered. If it has stopped moving forward it may start moving forward again providing it does so within 5 seconds. If the maul stops moving forward a second time and if the ball is being moved and the referee can see it, again a reasonable time is allowed for the ball to emerge. What constitutes 'reasonable' is always difficult to define, so use some discretion if the ball is clearly visible and one side has clearly won it, allow them to clear the maul.

One of the biggest problems with the maul for the referee is determining when it has been illegally collapsed - pulled down by the team not in possession as a destructive measure - and when it has been legally turned into a ruck by a player getting the ball on to the deck. It is illegal to collapse the maul, and the Law also says that, if the ball-carrier in a maul goes to ground and the ball is not immediately available for the continuation of play, a scrum should be ordered. Players wrestling for the ball in a maul may try and bring the ball-carrier down as well, and this should be prevented by the referee. It is also illegal to attempt to drag opponents out of the maul; this is particularly common when players believe that opponents are in an offside position. If they are offside the referee should penalise them but, quite often, they are there legally because they have come into a tackle from the opponents' side. In this situation the referee should shout 'He's there legally; leave him alone!'.

2.3 Positioning at ruck and maul

To manage rucks and mauls effectively, the referee must get to the breakdown quickly in anticipation of a ruck or maul being formed, and he has two main priorities. He must determine the exact position of the ball, and he must encourage all participants to stay on their feet.

Clearly, in situations where a ruck or maul is formed as a result of a tackle, the referee will be particularly concerned about the safety of players on the ground, and he must be especially vigilant about use of the boot. There is a widely held misconception that it is a player's right to ruck these grounded people out of the way of the ball with their feet. Not only is this illegal, it is also highly dangerous; it is the referee's duty to look after those players and, wherever possible, to make them move away as quickly as possible.

Having moved in close to the ruck/maul to locate the ball, the referee should move away and take up a position where he can still see the ball but can also get a better all-round view of play (*see* **Figure 1**). In most cases this is best achieved by moving towards the side more likely to win the ball and facing the other side, at an angle, so as to observe offside by both participants and non-participants. Don't be afraid to move all the way around the ruck/maul in your effort to keep track of the ball, but be aware of where you are standing so that you do not obstruct the players - and, once you've located the ball, you don't need to keep on circling the ruck/maul for the sake of it.

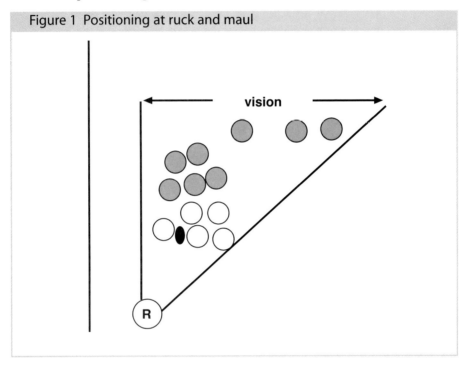

Figure 1 Positioning at ruck and maul

2.4 Offside at ruck and maul

The offside line at rucks and mauls is defined as: *a line parallel to the goal-line through the hindmost foot of the player's team in the ruck or maul.*

Essentially, players must not join a ruck or maul from their opponents' side, or in front of the hindmost player of his team in the ruck/maul (which means that they can join level with the hindmost player having come from behind the offside line). Additionally, players who are not participating must retire behind the offside line and stay there until the ruck/maul is finished. Players who are in the ruck/maul and then unbind must also retire behind the offside line (*see* **Figure 2**).

Referees should also pay attention to obstruction, or shielding. This occurs when a player at the back of a ruck/maul takes the ball and begins a new move-ment by backing into his own players rather than letting them join on to him

Figure 2 Offside at ruck and maul

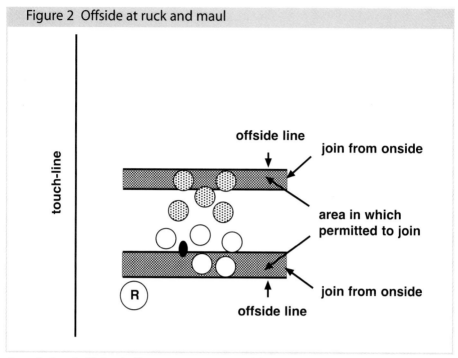

from behind. If the ball-carrier is protected by a wall of his own players, they are obstructing the opposition and must be penalised.

Rucks and mauls which are formed at the line-out have a similar offside line, subject to the caveat that participants in the line-out do not have to join the ruck/maul but must observe the other offside lines of the line-out. The referee needs to watch for two offences here, at the front and the back of a line-out.

Firstly, the participants at the back of a line-out may choose not to join the ruck/maul, but they must not leave the corridor of the line-out, especially when they drop away past the 15-metre line. If they move beyond that line, and the line-out is still in progress, they must retire 10 metres. Secondly, the opponent of the player throwing in the ball may decide not to join the ruck/maul, and they must not stray over the offside line of that ruck or maul.

2.5 Major offences at ruck and maul

A player joining the ruck must have his head and shoulders no lower than his hips, and he must bind on with at least one arm around the body of a player of his own team who is in the ruck. This means that a player who is in a ruck, but who is not binding on his own players, is there illegally and should be penalised if he interferes with play.

The only way to get the ball out of a ruck is with the feet: use of the hands or legs is illegal (with the exception of the scrum-half or hindmost player as previously mentioned). Players on the ground must not interfere with the ball and must make every effort to roll away from it. It is also illegal to drag away an opponent who is lying on the ground in a ruck. Wilful collapsing of a ruck, and falling over or kneeling, are penalty kick offences.

Most major offences at the maul are the same as for the ruck, with the exception that a participant does not have to bind as long as he is caught in or bound to the maul by other players: if he is in this position he should be protected as other players may think he is offside. Say, 'He's OK', or blow quickly to prevent offences.

2.6 Ruck and maul - referee's checklist

The key elements of successful ruck and maul management are as follows.
- Players remain on their feet, with wilful collapsing penalised.
- Players join level with or behind the hindmost player.
- Dangerous play - especially rucking of players lying on the ground - is severely dealt with.
- Offside by participants and non-participants is observed and prevented.
- Participants are correctly bound.
- Heads and shoulders are no lower than hips.
- Consistent application to allow the ball to emerge from static mauls.
- Obstruction/shielding is penalised.
- Handling in the ruck is penalised.

3 Advantage

By now it will have become obvious that the referee has an enormous amount of discretion written into the 21 Laws. Of all the Laws, Law 8 (Advantage) gives the referee the most scope to exercise this discretion. A note to this Law even states: *The referee has wide discretion when making decisions. The referee is the sole judge of whether a team has gained an advantage. Advantage can be either tactical or territorial.*

In a typical match there are so many infringements that the referee could be blowing the whistle almost continuously. Although this might show a good knowledge of the Laws, it is not what the game of rugby is all about, and such a referee would be not be demonstrating any understanding of, or feeling for, the game. The players want to play, and they are dependent on the common sense of the referee to let them. The advantage Law is therefore a critical area.

Many advantage situations are clear-cut: a player knocks on accidentally, an opponent recovers the ball and gains territory as a result - no need to blow for the original infringement as the non-offending team has won a benefit. But players don't always realise that advantage is being played - and, somewhat surprisingly, they don't always appreciate it even if they do know. Take that last example: the non-offending team might prefer to have a scrum in their favour, rather than let play continue, because they are dominant up front and would prefer a set-piece move from the scrum. Is it the referee's job to analyse and understand this? It probably isn't, although he must be sympathetic to the temper of the game and its structure. He also has to consider, above all else, the safety of the players, and advantage should not be played if he thinks that is in jeopardy.

So the referee needs to think not just about **territorial** advantage, but also **tactical** advantage. Say, for instance, that a penalty kick infringement is spotted by the referee inside the non-offending team's 22-metre area. He lets play continue because the defending team is in possession of the ball and has an opportunity to gain an advantage. The ball is kicked to touch in front of the place where the infringement occurred. Now the referee has to decide whether an advantage has actually been gained, because the mere opportunity is not sufficient. The offending team will have the throw-in. Is that fair, or should the non-offending team be awarded a penalty kick so that, if the kicker finds touch, his side will have the resulting throw-in? Law 8 states: *Advantage must be clear and real.* It is up to the referee to decide how to interpret this.

As a guide, unless a team has demonstrated a willingness to run the ball from any position, including behind their own goal-line, the referee will normally award a penalty immediately for any relevant offence which takes place within the non-offending team's 22-metre area.

There are few easy decisions about advantage, and each case has to be judged on its merits. If the referee has an empathy with the game, and knows the strengths and weaknesses of each side, he will be much better placed to decide on when to play advantage and when not. Above all, he must be consistent in his application of this Law for both sides.

The primary advantage signal - one arm outstretched at waist height in the direction of the non-offending team - is not particularly well known by players or spectators. It is very helpful for the referee to shout, 'Advantage to Reds', as he outstretches his arm: the players then know that you've seen the infringement and are trying to let the match flow. For penalty kick offences, good referees will tell the non-offending side that they have seen the infringement, and that they will penalise the offending team if no advantage is subsequently gained. It also helps to remind the players to play to the whistle, rather than to stop as soon as they've spotted what they think is an infringement.

But for how long should you allow the non-offending team to try and gain an advantage? Is it three seconds, five seconds, or even longer? Again, this depends on the nature of the match, and can only be decided when you're on the pitch and in the middle of the action. You will know if advantage should be applied; you will have a good idea of whether the non-offending team has any chance of gaining from their opponents' infringements; and you will be able to judge whether the players appreciate a longer or shorter advantage period. Use your common sense: referees should not play advantage when the ball has become static - especially in tackle situations - and there is a well organised defence. Don't play advantage for the sake of it.

When you feel that a team has sufficient opportunities for an advantage, return your outstretched arm to your side and shout 'Advantage over'. Then there can be no doubt that the advantage period has finished.

Advantage is therefore strongly linked to your understanding of the game, and your appreciation of what the players are trying to achieve. How you read the game will affect your decisions regarding advantage.

There are three restrictions on the use of advantage by the referee, and neither team may gain an advantage from the following.

- When the ball or a player carrying it touches the referee.
- When the ball emerges from either end of a scrummage tunnel.
- When there is an irregularity in play that is not provided for in the Laws (e.g. a dog runs on to the pitch and bites a player!).

There's one other point to remember: the referee has to strike the right balance between playing advantage and ensuring that players conform to the Laws through his use of appropriate sanctions. Especially in the first 10 minutes of a game, referees are setting out their stall, conditioning the players so that they know what to expect if they infringe. A good understanding of the game, however, may allow you to play advantage from the very first whistle, providing you let all the players know you are in control.

3.1 Advantage - referee's checklist

- Advantage is played giving due consideration to the temper of the game and the safety of the players.
- Advantage is applied consistently.
- Recognition that, in many cases, the penalty kick is the major advantage, especially in defensive positions.
- Consistent verbal and hand communication that advantage is being played, and that advantage had been played.

4 Open play

The term 'open play' covers a multitude of situations and is mainly concerned with what happens before or after a scrum, line-out, restart kick, tackle, ruck or maul.

In open play, the referee has to be positioned well to spot infringements and, wherever possible, to prevent them through clear and concise instructions. Players, coaches, spectators and referees share a desire to see a good, open game in which both sides can play to their full potential; the referee is pivotal in ensuring that this happens through his positioning, skill, discretion and judgement. Being in the right place, and having a global view of the game, are vital to achieve this.

4.1 Positioning in open play

New referees often have a major problem in knowing where to be for any particular situation, especially if they have taken up the whistle after a long career as a player. Running lines for referees are completely different from those for players, and a good referee rarely stands still: he is constantly looking for the optimal position to see the ball and the majority of the players. If he is too close to the action, he runs the risk of missing infringements and, in the worst case, obstructing players.

There are three elements which help the referee to keep up with play:
- his angles of running
- his change of pace
- his awareness.

4.1.1 Angles of running

Wherever possible, the referee needs to take the direct route to follow play. The direct route does not always mean the shortest route: short cuts can cause serious problems. For example, the ball comes out of a scrum and the scrum-half goes down the blind-side, with you standing on the open-side. The short cut might be to come round the back of the scrum of the opposing side, anticipating that you will get in front of play on the blind side. But, in doing this, you are immediately blocked by the defending back row as they break off and you are unable to see what the blind-side flanker and winger are doing to defend against the scrum-half's action.

A better route would be to follow the scrum-half around his own side of the scrum, even though this means you are behind play. With this positioning, you will at least have a better chance to see infringements and to monitor the defending players' actions. Following the passage of the ball and the ball-carrier is therefore key.

Angles of running for the referee are all about diagonals. Remember how you should position yourself at set-pieces, slightly angled to the play so that you can see both the ball and the majority of the players. Running lines follow the same principle, so that you are working almost diagonally to the passage of play. You need to be able to see forward passes, knock-ons, offsides, and dangerous play, and you need to be able to look behind you to see what's going on as the set-piece breaks up. A diagonal running line helps you to achieve all this. Bear in mind, too, that you will be watching your touch judges for their signals.

4.1.2 Change of pace

At set pieces, such as a scrum or line-out, be on your toes and ready to move off quickly, rapidly changing up 'through the gears' so as to keep up with play as soon as the ball emerges. This, of course, can only happen if you are fit and have worked on your acceleration and sprinting: you must have that initial burst of energy to enable you to get to the ball quickly without the effort resulting in a loss of concentration.

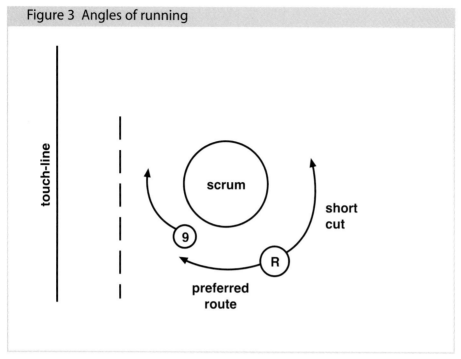

Figure 3 Angles of running

4.1.3 Awareness

The good referee will also use his awareness to make reasoned predictions on the choices available to players in open play. Are they most likely to kick, to pass, or to run? Which way will they go? You cannot always accurately anticipate where play will go, but you do need to be aware of the most likely options so that, whichever one is taken, it will not surprise you and leave you flat-footed and out of position.

4.1.4 Near the goal-line

Nowhere is good positioning more critical than near the goal-line. Events which take place in or near the in-goal area are crucial to the result of the game and, more than anywhere else on the field, the referee will be expected by the players to get it right here and to communicate decisions clearly, quickly and confidently.

First of all, you have to be very clear about what the in-goal area is: *In-goal is the area bounded by a goal-line, touch-in-goal-lines and dead-ball line. It includes the goal-line and goal posts but excludes touch-in-goal-lines and dead-ball line.* This means that a touch-down or try can be made on the goal-line, or against a goal post.

For the referee, there are several factors to bear in mind when play is near the in-goal area.

- He must be aware of where the goal-line is and cross it in advance of play wherever possible, **except** at a moving maul where he should keep the ball in view.
- He must be a little in front of play and, if necessary, be prepared to take short cuts from a ruck, maul or set-piece in order to see the ball being grounded.
- He must get as close as possible to the point of touch-down without getting in the way.
- He must be prepared for the unexpected (remembering that a drop-goal may be attempted and he needs to be well positioned for it).
- He must take careful note of who last played the ball before it goes into the in-goal area, because this will determine the restart after the ball is dead if no other offence occurs.
- He must remember that, for most offences in-goal, the penalty is the same as for a similar offence within the field of play (except that tackle, ruck, maul, scrummage and line-out can only take place in the field of play).

If there is any doubt about whether the ball has been grounded on or beyond the goal-line, the referee should award a 5-metre scrum to the attacking team. Near the goal-line is also the area where the penalty try is most often awarded. A penalty try, which is awarded under the posts, is given in a situation where, but for foul play by the defending team, a try would **probably** have been scored, or it would **probably** have been scored in a more favourable position (i.e. nearer the posts) than that where the ball was grounded. Don't forget that, if you award a try and you are abused by the defending players, you are within your rights to award a penalty kick to the opposition as the restart from the half-way line.

Positioning in open play is therefore a combination of factors.

- Following the passage of the ball and ball-carrier (in preference to taking a short cut).
- Gaining sight lines not blocked by other players, and avoiding blind spots.
- A preference for in-field positions rather than touch-side.
- Close attention to play on or near the goal-line.
- Avoiding looking directly at the sun.
- Anticipation of the flow of the game - through a tactical appreciation - to ensure you stay in a good position.

4.2 Offside in open play

Offside is one of the most important components of refereeing open play. The Law states that a player is offside in open play when in front of a team-mate who has the ball or last played the ball. A player who is offside in this way is out of the game until put onside again, and must not take any further part in the game or move towards opponents waiting to play the ball.

How is a player put onside? There are four ways in which he can be put onside by his own team.

- The team-mate, with the ball, runs past and in front of him.
- The team-mate behind, who has kicked the ball, runs past and in front of him.
- Any other team-mate, who was onside when the ball was kicked, runs past and in front of him.
- The offside player runs back behind onside team-mates.

Figure 4   Onside by own team

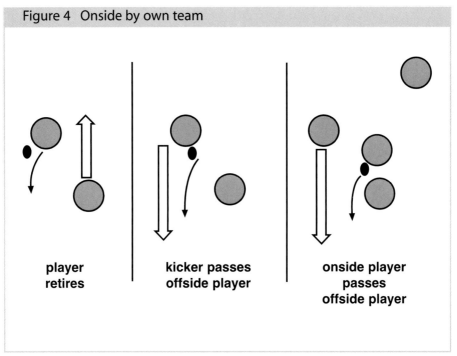

| player retires | kicker passes offside player | onside player passes offside player |

If the ball is kicked, and an offside player is within 10 metres of the opponent waiting to catch the ball, he must move out of the 10-metre area or be penalised, because he cannot be put onside by any of his own players. A quick shout of 'Retire!' when the ball is kicked forward will remind offside players of this obligation.

Figure 5   Offside: 10-metre zone

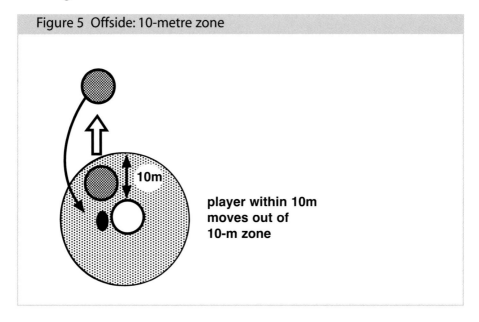

player within 10m moves out of 10-m zone

Opponents can put an offside player onside in three ways:
- by running 5 metres with the ball
- by kicking or passing the ball
- by intentionally touching, but not holding, the ball.

The important thing to remember about offside in open play is that there is no penalty for the offence unless the offside player does something negative, like obstructing an opponent or moving towards the opponents waiting to play the ball. You should also differentiate between deliberate and accidental offside, and you should, wherever possible, allow the non-offending team to try and gain an advantage.

The penalty for deliberate offside is a penalty kick where the player was first offside or, at the option of the non-offending team, a scrummage at the place where the ball was last played by the offending team. In the situation where more than one offside player move towards the opponents, or to the place where the ball pitches, the mark for the penalty will be that of the offside player closest to the player waiting for the ball or where the ball pitches.

4.3 Open play - referee's checklist

You should be concentrating on the following elements in open play.

- Management of offside, especially from kicks ahead, looking at the 10-metre exclusion zone, forward movement, and players in front of the kicker.
- Obstruction in open play, including shielding of players and crossing (where a player walks in front of a team-mate carrying the ball to protect him from a tackle).
- Positioning for play near the goal-line.
- Positioning to see knock-ons and forward passes.
- Positioning for dropped goals.

CHAPTER 4

Restarts

For the purist, restarts from the scrum and line-out remain the most fascinating part of the game. Seeing the packs in a close physical contest is exciting and these set-pieces, when properly managed, are one of the highlights of rugby.

For the referee, there are several challenges in managing restarts - **scrum, line-out, kick-off, drop-kick, penalty and free kicks**. Above all, the way in which a referee manages the situation just before a restart is critical to whether this phase of play is successful or not. Preventive refereeing is the key - stop players from infringing before a restart and you are much more likely to exercise the necessary control and to avoid flash-points.

1 The scrum

The scrum is one of the classic set-pieces of rugby. It is also, from the referee's perspective, one of the most difficult to manage. There are numerous possible areas for infringement, not only by the participants but also by the backs. It is probably fair to say that the scrum presents the referee with his most challenging tasks as regards safety of players: there are significant potential dangers for front rows that are badly set or mismatched, and the referee will ensure that all possible steps are taken to avoid injury to the players.

The scrum Laws (Law 20) are specifically designed with safety in mind, and the referee needs to pay particular attention to all aspects and to abide by the letter of the Laws in this area. A well managed scrum is an absolute prerequisite for a good game, as it is the most frequently used method of restarting the game after an infringement. For the scrum to be managed well, the referee needs to establish his standards from the start; in fact, this is an area that he should consider telling the players about before they go out on to the pitch. If you tell the front rows in advance exactly what your setting procedure will be, there is less scope for misunderstanding once the match has begun. Having set your standards, the referee must them implement them in the match.

Scrums normally result from what can be described as non-destructive infringements - accidental knock-ons, forward passes, static mauls, trapped ball in the ruck, for example - and are awarded to the non-offending side or otherwise according to the Laws. The game is restarted at the mark where the infringement occurred, unless the Laws allow for alternatives (e.g. so that the feet of all participants remain in play, line-out infringements where the mark is on the 15-metre line, illegal drop-outs and restart kicks, infringements in the in-goal area). The referee signals the nature of the infringement, the award of a scrum and the side which has the throw-in. He also makes a mark with his boot to show the central line of the scrum, around which the two packs should set themselves. It is also useful to set the two *hookers* over the mark in order to help the referee set the scrum square.

Typically there are four different kinds of scrum, and you may - if you're very unlucky - encounter all of them in the same match.

- Positive.
- Negative.
- Passive.
- Destructive.

1.1 The positive scrum

In the positive scrum the dominant pack will set itself correctly, with shoulders parallel to the ground and all eight participants facing directly forward. They will shove in a straight line and push their opposition backwards without trying to disrupt the scrum through any illegal manoeuvres. You are most likely to see an example of a positive scrum when there is a put-in for the attacking team on the 5-metre line or close to the goal-line. Your primary concern in this situation is to ensure that the opposing participants are safe and are not infringing and, when near the goal-line, to position yourself so that you can clearly see when and if the ball reaches the goal-line. This is because the scrum ends once it is on or over the goal-line and, of course, there is likely to be a touch-down in this scenario.

1.2 The negative scrum

Players, coaches and referees often refer to 'the secrets of the front-row union'. Even if you have been a front-row player yourself, it is very difficult as a referee to spot all the actual infringements which occur in this area, however much you may suspect illegal actions. However, there are various signs which tell you that one or both front rows are engaged in a negative scrum, and various ways of preventing it.

Much of the negative activity can be obviated by proper setting of the front rows. The recommended sequence for engagement of the front rows is: **crouch, pause, engage**. The Law confirms this: *Before commencing engagement each front row must be in a crouched position with heads and shoulders no lower than their hips and so that they are within one arm's length of the opponents' shoulders. In the interests of safety, each front row should engage in the sequence of crouch, then pause and only engage on the call 'Engage' given by the referee.* (In under-19 rugby, this sequence is extended so that it becomes: **crouch, touch, pause, engage**.)

A negative scrum starts when one or both front rows decide to hinder this process. A front row may be in the crouch position but does not line up heads and shoulders at the same level and angle. This makes it much more difficult for their opponents to engage against them. Additionally, the hooker may obstruct the tight-head prop by moving his head so that the prop cannot put his head in the space between the hooker and his loose-head prop.

By getting the front rows to set and engage precisely as the Law demands, there is much less opportunity for negative scrummaging, and the referee needs to get this right from the first scrum. It is therefore quite acceptable to tell the skippers before the game exactly how you intend to set the scrums, and what sequence of commands you will use. At the adult game it is vital to say CROUCH, HOLD then ENGAGE. A correct engagement is the secret to a successful scrum.

1.3 The passive scrum

There will be passages in the match where both packs decide that they will simply lean into the scrum without applying any major force. This can occur after prolonged periods of open play, when one or both packs are very tired, or when the scrum takes place in midfield and there is no particular danger or potential advantage from the position. Problems may occur here if one pack then decides to put on a shove, in which case the passive pack will be caught off guard and may well collapse, or resort to negative or destructive tactics to prevent it.

1.4 The destructive scrum

Even if you manage to set the scrum well, you still face significant potential problems if one or both packs - especially the front rows - decide to employ destructive tactics to hinder an effective and legal process.

There are two relevant Laws here.

Law 20 states: *Players in the front rows must not at any time during the scrummage wilfully adopt a position, or take any action, by twisting or lowering the body or by pulling on an opponent's dress, which is likely to cause the scrummage to collapse.*

Law 26 (Foul Play) states: *It is illegal for any player:*

- *in the front row of a scrummage to form down some distance from the opponents and rush against them*
- *in the front row of a scrummage wilfully to lift an opponent off his feet or force him upwards out of the scrummage*
- *wilfully to cause a scrummage, ruck or maul to collapse.*

It should be noted that the penalties for Law 10 infringements are severe; the referee is instructed either to order the offending player off or to caution him that he will be ordered off if he repeats the offence. This is obviously in addition to the award of a penalty or penalty try.

You can tell a good deal about participants' intentions by looking at their body positions and, as importantly, the placing of their feet and the angle of their legs. If the shoulders are above, or level with, the hips, the thighs vertical, and the knees bent at the angle needed to maintain this position, a forward shove is effectively produced, and there is less likely to be a problem in the front row (*see* **Figure 6**). When any or all of these positions are not in evidence, this is a signal that destructive tactics may be under consideration. The challenge for referees is to spot who is infringing; in some cases a front row player may be innocent but is forced into a poor position by the actions of his opponent.

Figure 6 Body positions of front row

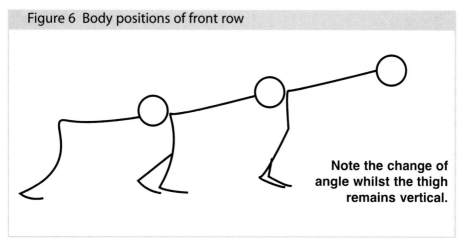

Note the change of angle whilst the thigh remains vertical.

Possibly the easiest infringement to spot is **pulling down**. This occurs when a prop (usually the tight-head) binds to his opponent with his outside arm so that he is exerting a downward pressure. It is easy to spot because, with his arm bent, his elbow will either be pointing towards the ground or upwards. However, some very strong props will still be able to exert a downward pressure with the elbow straight: in this case the forearm will be pointing downwards. Pulling down is a penalty offence, as it is extremely dangerous and destructive. The outside arms of the props must be as level as possible, and it is the referee's duty to keep the elbows up and the wrists level. Ideally, a prop's forearm should be parallel to the ground.

The tight-head prop may also engage so that his body position is driving towards the shoulder and head of the opposing prop - the manoeuvre known as **boring**. This again is a penalty offence. To spot this, the referee should take a position which allows him to see over the top of the set scrum; from this angle he can check whether the tight-head props are in a position for 'an effective forward shove'. Clearly, it is preferable if the referee takes preventive measures, asking the props to straighten up if it appears that they are not set properly.

Collapsing the scrum can be caused by other methods apart from pulling down and boring. These include pulling the leg of a prop, either by the opposing prop or flanker - this offence is very serious and warrants at least a caution for the offending player. Be alert to the binding of the loose-head prop, who may get under the opposing tight-head and pull down. A hooker can also collapse the scrum by getting his head lower than his hips and driving downwards with his back bent. These actions are normally accompanied by a change of angle at the knee - the knee is driven forward so that the thigh ceases to be vertical (*see* **Figure 7**). Collapsing the scrum is obviously a very dangerous manoeuvre and must be penalised - again, preventive action can be taken by the referee so that all the players are set for the forward shove and comply with the legal body positions.

Figure 7 Change of front row body position

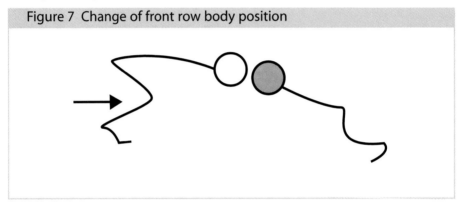

Another dangerous scrum offence occurs when one pack dips slightly once the ball is in the scrum and then rises, shoving upwards instead of forwards and getting underneath the opposing front row so that it is unable to stay crouched and its bindings break. Once the engagement has been broken the scrum is at an end, but that may not stop the offending team from continuing to push. The 'dip and drive' manoeuvre is legal, however, as long as the resulting drive is straight ahead rather than upwards.

Bear in mind that **wheeling** the scrum is not an offence, even though it may cause problems. The scrum must not wheel more than 90 degrees from its original position: when it does, the scrum is reformed and the put-in goes to the side who had gained possession or otherwise by the same team. This is another area where the scrum must be kept square at put-in time and not at angle of 20% in order to assist the wheel.

Although the majority of destructive tactics in the scrum are employed by the front row, you must also pay attention to the back row. The flankers are allowed to bind at any angle to the pack, but they are not allowed to change their position once the ball has been put in. This Law stops them from swinging out to obstruct the opposing scrum half as he follows the ball round to the back of the scrum. Additionally, the flankers are not allowed to bind on opposing players with their outer arms, which is a free kick infringement. Nor must flankers bind through the props legs, they must bind onto the 2nd row.

The referee must also check that the back rows stay bound until the scrum is over. Law 20, (6), (d) states: *All players in a scrum, other than those in a front row, must bind with at least one arm and hand around the body of another player of the same team.* This means that the whole arm, from wrist to shoulder, must be bound. Back row players can put their heads up as long as they stay bound. The number eight can also bind in three different positions at the back (*see* **Figure 8**); there is no obligation in Law for him to put his head between the locks. Again, a few well chosen words - 'Stay bound' - will help to keep the back row legal.

1.5 Scrum management

To achieve control of the scrum, the referee needs to be alert to all the potential problems listed above - and one of the best ways of managing the scrum is to be in the right place. Positioning at the scrum is particularly important because the referee also needs to have a clear view of the backs. The challenge

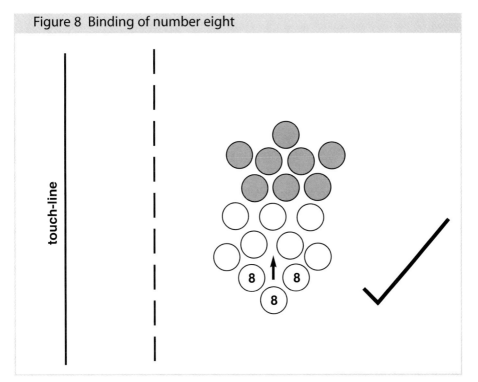

Figure 8 Binding of number eight

touch-line

8 8
8

Figure 9 Positioning of referee during a scrum

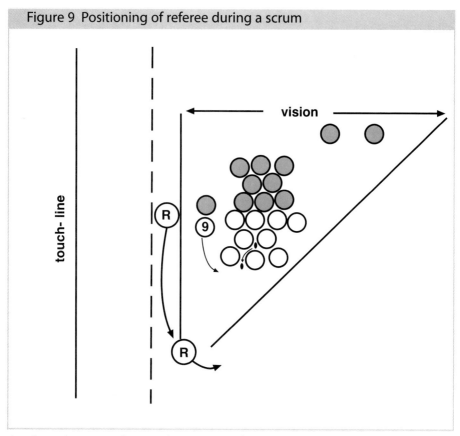

for the referee is to know where to stand to get the broadest possible view so that he can watch the actions of the packs and still be properly positioned to see whether the backs are encroaching beyond the onside line.

When setting the front rows before they have engaged, the referee will normally stand at the side of the scrum from which the ball will be put in (and remember that there is no restriction on which side is used). Do not stand directly between the front rows; they don't like this as they want to look at the opponents and see where they are going to engage - and you are liable to be caught in the middle when they do engage. Instead, stand close by the side and hold one or both arms outstretched into the space between the front rows and say 'Crouch and Hold'. When they are crouched and you give your signal - 'Engage', for example - you take away your arm to give them a further signal that they can engage. If you use your left hand and stand to the left side you will not delay the _____ from putting in the ball.

At this point you must move away quickly so that the scrum-half has access to the tunnel. Pull away to the side and turn so that you are almost facing the team which does not have the put-in, but do not step back too much because

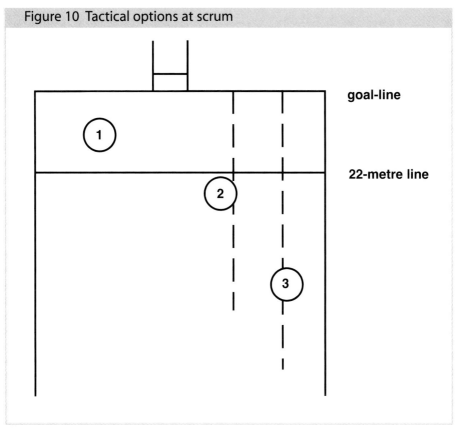

Figure 10 Tactical options at scrum

goal-line

22-metre line

you want to be watching the tunnel for a crooked feed and foot-up. At the first few scrums you may want to remind the scrum-half that he is obliged to put in the ball without delay - 'Straight in, scrum-half' - so that he knows what you want. Delaying the put-in is a free kick offence; it is normally the hooker who signals the timing of the put-in and, if he is delaying his signal, then make sure you have a word to get him to speed up the process. Once you are satisfied that the ball has gone in straight, you should stay in your original position for just a few moments to check on the behaviour of the front rows.

If there appear to be problems on the other side of the scrum, ask the scrum-half to hold the ball until you've got round there to identify what those problems are. You can always set the scrum from 'the wrong side' if the need arises. Remember that the good referee is a manager and a problem-solver, so go to where the problem is and get the players to take responsibility for implementing your solution to the problem.

You should follow the ball as it moves to the back of the pack which has won the ball, far enough away from the side of the scrum so that both scrum-halves can move around without interference (*see* **Figure 9**). You need to be here to watch the flanker to see if his body position changes to obstruct the opposing scrum-half, and you're also well positioned to check on the backs for offside. Additionally, you need to be alert to back row players unbinding before the scrum is over.

Keep on checking the front rows for destructive actions and, as the ball reaches the back of the scrum, begin to move towards midfield, making sure that you do not limit the options of the number eight and the scrum-half by standing in an obstructive position. With this in mind, you may choose to stand on the 'wrong' side of the scrum if it is very close to the touch-line; this will then allow the scrum-half to kick for touch without having to get the ball past you, and it will position you better if he passes it to a receiving player for an

At scrum 1, what is the most likely option the attacking team will take:
• push over?
• number eight drive for the line?
• crash ball at centre?

Are these options more likely than:
• miss-out pass to outside centre, with full-back in the line?
• miss-out pass to outside centre, miss-out pass beyond full-back to wing?

If this is the range of possibilities, think about where you would next want to be, to be close to the action.

At scrum 2, what is the most likely next point of attack:
• blind through 8, 9 and 11?
• open through 8, releasing to 6 to run at defending 10 and 12?
• open through centre field?

If this is in descending order of likelihood, where would you like to be when the next action develops?

And, at scrum 3, what's more likely:
• box kick by 9?
• pass to 10, bomb to defending 15?
• back row infield, ruck/maul/release outside backs?

attempted drop-goal.

From **Figure 9** you can see that the recommended movement and positioning of the referee allow him a clear path to the next phase of play without obstructing the players, and that he can see both the scrum and the backs.

Be aware of the effect that field position may have on subsequent play. Look at the three scrum positions in **Figure 10** and consider how play is most likely to develop for the attacking side after a successful scrum.

Again, by making some prejudgement (which could be wrong, but more often than not is likely to be right), you can anticipate the next point of action, and be there.

Don't stop refereeing the scrum as soon as the ball is out. The scrum is a potential flash-point and front row players may have more interest in resolving private battles than in getting to the next break-down. Many infringements occur when the referee's back is turned, so be vigilant of the scrum break up. Here it obviously helps if you have a touch judge.

1.6 Offside at the scrum

There are three offside lines at the scrum: two lines parallel to the goal-lines through the hindmost foot of the players in the scrum, and the line through the position of the ball (*see* **Figure 11**). The two 'hindmost foot' lines are for the

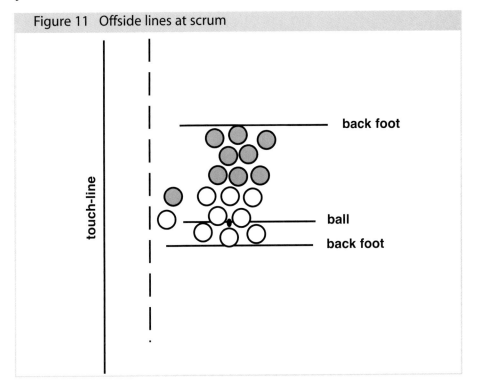

Figure 11   Offside lines at scrum

backs to observe: they cannot move up beyond that line whilst the scrum is in progress. The 'ball' line is for the scrum-half whose side has not won the ball: as he moves round the scrum to follow the ball back he must not place either foot in front of the ball. This player must also stay in 'close proximity' to the scrum; this means that, if he moves away from the scrum to adopt a defensive position, he must retire behind the 'hindmost foot' offside line.

1.7 The scrum - referee's checklist

To recap, here are the referee's key priorities for effective management of the scrum.

- He follows the correct engagement procedures: front row bodies parallel to the touch-line; front row in pushing position; heads straight; binding correct; scrum stationary; head and shoulders above hips.
- He controls scrum engagement by saying 'Crouch', 'hold' and 'engage' – when the referee says 'engage' the two front rows join together.
- He interferes minimally if the scrum is stable and working.
- He manages the collapsed scrum.
- The ball is put in immediately, straight and at the correct distance.
- He observes offside by participants, including back rows remaining bound until the scrum is over.
- He observes offside by non-participants.

Additionally, the referee should do the following.

- Set the scrum in the correct position and place.
- Ensure the scrum-half is 1 metre from the scrum.
- Prevent the opposing scrum-half from touching the scrum.
- Prevent flankers from swinging out.
- Take preventive action.
- Take punitive action by penalising.
- Position himself to achieve all of the above.

Note Remember that the Laws for under-19 rugby vary quite significantly for the scrum, both in terms of managing the engagement and in the way the participating players form the scrum. There are also variations on wheeling, the distance the scrummage can move with the ball in, as well as restrictions on the scrum-halves at under-15 level. Referees must familiarise themselves with these variations.

2 The line-out

Before looking at the line-out - and the quick throw-in - we need to consider the issue of the ball in touch.

According to Law 19 (Touch and Line-out), the ball is in touch:

- when it is not being carried by a player and it touches a touch-line or the ground or a person or object on or beyond it.
- when it is carried by a player and it or the player carrying it touches a touch-line or the ground beyond it.

2.1 Touch

It's important to understand these definitions, because there are circumstances in which the ball can cross the plane of the touch-line but not be in touch. For example, if the ball is kicked to touch and it crosses the plane of the touch-line and then recrosses back into the field of play, without having landed or touched anything beyond the touch-line, the ball did not go into touch. Additionally, a player with both feet in the playing area can catch, deflect or tap the ball, even when it has crossed the plane of the touch-line, and keep the ball in play as long as both his feet remain in the playing area.

With touch judges, the referee's job in making decisions about touch is substantially easier. Without them, the referee must apply common sense - and, as mentioned earlier, he will already have made it clear to the teams that he is not there to run the line.

2.2 Quick throw-in

The simple fact that the ball has gone into touch does not mean that a line-out will follow. Subject to certain restrictions, the side throwing in the ball can choose to take a quick throw-in, and the referee must be alert to this.

A quick throw-in is permissible under the following conditions.

- The ball that went into touch must be used, and it must only have been touched by the player throwing it in (so it cannot be given to him by another player or spectator), except that, where a player has been forced into touch with the ball in his possession, a quick throw-in by the opposition is allowed.

- The line-out must not have formed (a formed line-out consisting of at least two players from each team lining up in single lines parallel to the line of touch).

- The throw-in must be from any point along the touch-line between where the ball went into touch and the goal-line of the team throwing in the ball.

The touch judge will keep his flag raised, but will not put out his other arm in a horizontal position, if he adjudges that a quick throw-in is permissible. Once there are two players from each team, he should put out his other arm in a horizontal position.

For the quick throw-in to be valid, the ball must travel at least 5 metres straight along the line of touch before it hits the ground or is touched by another player; if it doesn't, then the opposing team has the choice of throwing in the ball or taking a scrum on the 15-metre line. If a player prevents it from going 5 metres, it is a free kick to the non-offending team.

2.3 Award of the throw-in

Normally the ball is thrown in by an opponent of the player whom it last touched, or by whom it was being carried before being in touch. The exception to this is the penalty kick: when the ball is kicked directly into touch from a penalty kick, the ball will be thrown in by the team which kicked the ball into touch.

The line of touch is an imaginary line across the field of play which runs at right angles to the touch-line through the place where the ball went into touch (or, in the case of a quick throw-in, where the ball is thrown in).

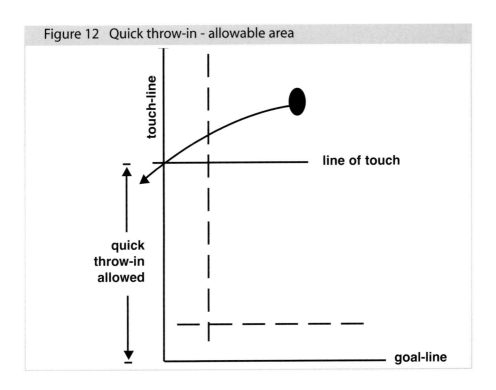

Figure 12 Quick throw-in - allowable area

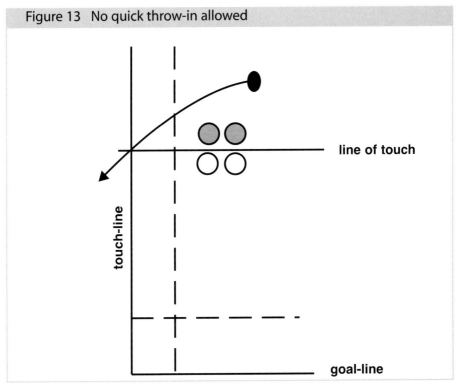

Figure 13 No quick throw-in allowed

The line of touch is determined as follows.

- From a penalty kick, or from a kick within 22 metres of the kicker's goal-line (including a free kick awarded within that area): at the place where it touched or crossed the touch-line.

- From a kick directly into touch other than as specified above, or when the kicker receives the ball outside his 22-metre line and retreats behind the line before kicking it or throws, knocks or kicks the ball back behind the line and retrieves it himself and kicks it: opposite the place from which the ball was kicked or at the place where it went into touch if that place is closer to the kicker's goal-line.

There are special Laws concerning drop-outs, kick-offs and restart kicks.

- If the ball is kicked directly into touch from a kick-off/restart, and the opposing team elects to accept the kick, the line-out is formed at the half-way line or where the ball went into touch, if that place is nearer to the kicker's goal-line.

- If the ball is kicked directly into touch from a drop-out, and the opposing team elects to accept the kick, the line-out is formed where the ball went into touch.

2.4 Formation of the line-out

Although a line-out has to be formed by at least two players from each side, there is no maximum. Theoretically, the side awarded the throw-in can choose to have 14 players in the line-out, as long as they are all within the zone between the 5- and 15-metre lines. The side throwing in determines the maximum number of players from either team who can participate; the opposition can have less, but not more, players. Be pragmatic about this: if players are genuinely making an effort to retire to the onside line when the line-out is shortened, don't automatically penalise them if the ball is thrown in whilst they are still offside, as long as they continue to retire and do not rejoin the line-out.

The two lines form on either side of the line of touch. The players must stand on their side half a metre from the line of touch, so that there is a 1 metre gap between the two lines (measured from shoulder to shoulder). This is a minimum and maximum measurement. The line-out stretches between the two lines - at 5 and 15 metres - which run parallel to the touch-line from which the ball is being thrown in.

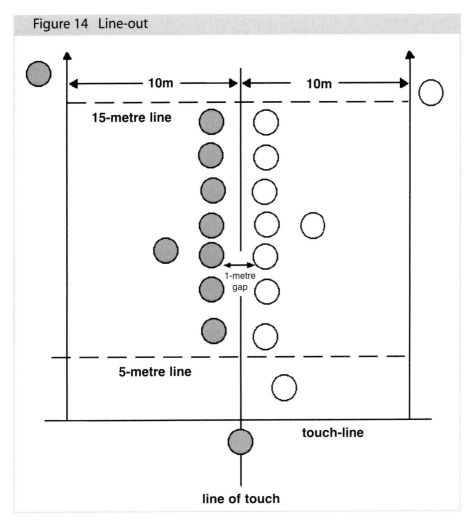

Figure 14 Line-out

The participants in the line-out are the two lines, the thrower and his immediate opponent, and the two players acting as scrum-half. Every other player is not participating at the line-out and must observe the Laws which govern them (see section 3.5).

Without touch judges, the referee has to monitor the formation of the line-out and ensure that there is a 1-metre gap and that the two lines are straight, i.e. parallel to the line of touch. To do this, the referee should stand on the line of touch at the front of the line-out as it is forming. The 1-metre gap is absolutely critical, because it gives the jumpers enough space to jump for the ball without infringement. Space at the line-out has to be the referee's major concern, so set the lines well. Enlist the help of the first men in each line - normally props - so that they know where you want them to stand. They can then hold their hands up to mark the line for their colleagues.

Most referees agree that walking along the gap is not a good idea: as likely as not the hooker will throw in the ball whilst you're standing in the middle and you'll be in big trouble. Referees should step to one side once they are satisfied that the line-out is properly formed (and *see* section 2.7 on positioning).

2.5 Offside at line-out

There are six offside lines at the line-out.

- The line of touch.
- The ball.
- The 5-metre line.
- The 15-metre line.
- 10 metres from the line of touch, parallel to the goal-lines, on either side of the line-out.

Participants are not allowed to cross the line of touch, unless they do so in the act of jumping for the ball and have started from their own side of the line of touch. They cannot take up a position in front of the ball unless they are carrying it or have tackled, or attempted to tackle, the ball carrier and they started the tackle from their side of the ball. They are not allowed to move beyond the 15-metre line until the ball has been released by the thrower, and then only if they are anticipating a long throw-in. The Law here is very specific: *If players so move and the ball is not thrown to or beyond them they must be penalised for offside.*

Referees talk about an imaginary corridor in which the line-out takes place. This corridor extends slightly beyond the outside shoulders of each line, between the 5- and 15-metre lines, and is the zone in which the line-out takes place. The reason for this corridor is to accommodate the 'peeling-off' manoeuvre, where one or more players move towards their own goal-line in anticipation of catching the ball when it has been passed or tapped back by one of their players in the line-out. Peeling-off is legal once the ball has left the hands of the player throwing it in. The corridor also allows players to move round behind their own line, once the ball has been thrown in, to form a maul. Within the corridor, and subject to the Laws' conditions, players can move without being offside.

Non-participants in the line-out have to stay behind the 10-metre offside line until the line-out has ended. Defining the end of a line-out is easy in theory, but difficult in practice.

> The Law says that the line-out ends when one of the following has happened.
>
> - A ruck or maul is taking place and all feet of players in the ruck or maul have moved beyond the line of touch.
> - A player carrying the ball leaves the line-out.
> - The ball has been passed, knocked back or kicked from the line-out.
> - The ball is thrown beyond a position 15 metres from the touch-line.
> - The ball becomes unplayable.

What tends to happen is that, as soon as the ball is thrown in, the defending backs move up, wrongly assuming that their offside line has moved to the back foot of an ensuing ruck or maul. To stop this keep a hand raised until the line out is over. If you have touch judges, then the touch judge on the far touch-line will take up a position on the offside line for the backs so that they can line up with him. But, if you don't have touch judges, you'll have to monitor this, so you need to enlist the help of the stand-offs. You should also be alert to the 'banana' line, where the stand-off and inside centre are onside, but the outside centre, wing and even full-back may encroach. It helps the players if you tell them your reading of the situation: 'It's not over, stay back!'. This isn't coaching; it's simply preventive refereeing.

2.6 Offences at the line-out

There are so many offences at the line-out that a whole book could probably be written on this single subject. The temptation for the referee is to decide that he will only concentrate on the most serious ones, and that those which do not interfere with play should be ignored. To an extent this attitude is permissible - other than for incidences of foul or dangerous play - because the Laws have been framed to encourage the ball to be recycled from the line-out as quickly as possible. If the ball comes away quickly and cleanly, and the 20-metre zone between the opposing backs is maintained, there is much more chance of an open, exciting game.

However, it is not the duty of the referee to encourage an open, exciting match at all costs. He has to make decisions and judgements about the nature of the infringements and the fairness with which the ball is won. If one side is consistently winning clean line-out ball, and moving it away quickly, you must consider why this is happening. Is it because of their technical superiority, or is it because they are deliberately impeding their opponents and stopping them from fair competition for the ball? If you don't look at this, you'll find 15 very angry players on the pitch.

As with most other aspects of the game, the Laws differentiate between what might be described as constructive and destructive infringements. For the participants, these are separated into across-the-line and along-the-line offences. The former take priority because they are likely to be destructive.

Across-the-line offences, which normally result in a penalty kick, occur when both sides of the line-out are involved. These include:
- offside
- using an opponent as a support when jumping for the ball
- holding, pushing, charging, obstructing or grasping an opponent not holding the ball.

Along-the-line offences, which normally result in a free kick, are related to only one side of the line-out. They include:
- peeling off and moving too far away from the line-out
- using another player of the same team as support when jumping for the ball
- lifting a player of the same team
- supporting any player of his own team before that player has jumped for the ball
- supporting a player of his own team below the waist (which is a penalty kick offence)
- standing within 5 metres of the touch-line or more than 15 metres from the touch-line until the ball has gone beyond them
- using the outside arm to play the ball, unless both hands are above the head
- closing the 1-metre gap, except when jumping for the ball.

Remember, too, that the non-participants can offend at the line-out by encroaching within the 10-metre offside line.

2.7 Positioning at the line-out

Where should the referee stand at a line-out? There is no one answer to this question. Some like to stand right at the front where they can see the gap and can make sure that the space for jumpers is protected. Others change their position for every line-out, especially once they're satisfied that the gap is being maintained and they can look for other offences. A few, especially vertically challenged referees, prefer to go to the back of the line-out and watch for across-the-line infringements.

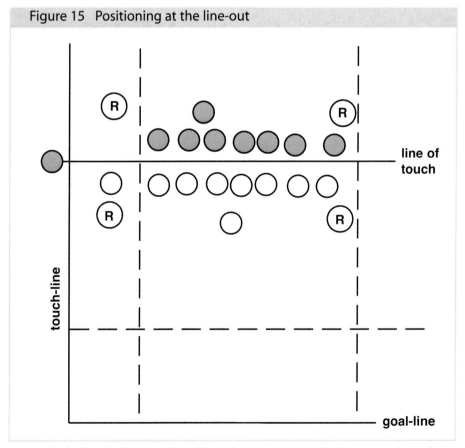

Figure 15 Positioning at the line-out

Because there are so many possible infringements at the line-out, the referee needs to decide what is important before he chooses his positioning. The gap must be set and maintained, so the referee needs to be close to the front of the line-out as it is forming. On a related point, the referee should be the first to the mark: it shows he is fit and keen and, more practically, he needs to be there in case there is a quick throw-in. As the line-out forms he is setting the standards; not only does he get the lines straight and properly separated, but he can also show the stand-offs where he judges their offside lines to be.

The line-out is also one of the few times when the referee can have a quiet word with players when the ball is out of play, and the opportunity should not be overlooked. 'Blue 6, I saw you offside at that last maul; don't do it again please'; 'Scrum-half, put the ball into the next scrum quicker, will you please?'. You have so few chances to let them know what you want, so take all of them. If necessary, tell the hooker not to throw in the ball until you're ready.

Never turn your back on the player throwing in the ball. You may think that you're still preparing the line-out, but he may think differently and release the ball before you're ready. If your back is turned, you won't be able to see if the throw is straight, or if it goes 5 metres, or if there is interference from his opposite number. Walk backwards away from him, and keep your body position angled so that you can see him, the line-out and the non-participants.

Early in the game you will probably want to stand at the front of the line-out. This enables you to see what's going on at the critical front positions: are the props obstructing each other?; illegally lifting their jumpers?; closing the gap?; or indulging in one of the many other tricks they can play? Are the jumpers staying on their marks or are they crossing the line? If possible, you should look into the eyes of these players so that they know you're watching them: you'd be amazed how their behaviour changes for the better if they know they're under scrutiny! Standing at the front of the line-out establishes your presence, even though it means you have to run further, and faster, when the ball gets out to the backs and into open play. Always stay on your toes so that you can move quickly to where the action is.

You should also avoid ball-watching: concentrate your vision on an area below the ball so that you are focussed on the likely contact areas between shoulder and hip. Some referees suggest that you should keep your chin on your chest to force yourself to look downwards: you can tell a lot about the intentions of the players by where their feet are and where they go. Of course you need to watch for the ball being thrown in straight, but you can judge that by the angle at which the jumper goes up to receive the ball. Do be alert to the fact that many subsequent infringements in the line-out - especially those across the line - occur as a result of a crooked throw, and that is the first offence.

If you decide to stand next to the jumpers, make sure that you do not get in the way of the scrum-half. Scrum-halves will not thank you for this and will waste no time in telling you if they think you're in the way.

Standing at the back of the line-out has some distinct advantages. You can see the ball as it is thrown in, watch for across-the-line offences, and are well posi-

Figure 16 Following the ball at the line-out

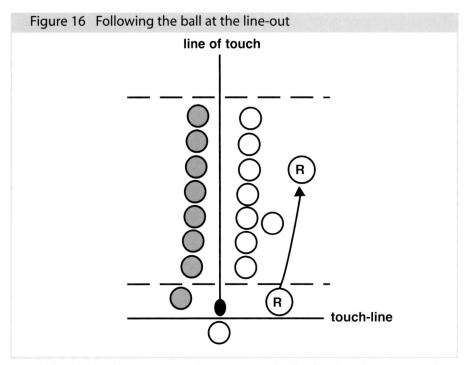

tioned both for a long throw and to monitor the backs. But this position does have its limitations, and it removes you from the immediate action which is more usually in the middle or towards the front of the line-out. It also separates you from the participants, giving them the impression that you don't care, or don't understand, what they get up to. If you want to go to the back, you should probably wait until you are completely satisfied that all is well in the line-out - or if you suspect that numbers six and seven are infringing. Once at the back, you must be very careful not to impede a long throw-in, and you've got to be sure that you'll be able to see a short throw-in to the front player in the line-out. If you have a touch judge, standing at the back is much less of a problem.

Finally, it is a general rule of thumb that you should stand on the throwing team's side of the line-out - but this is a rule which has many exceptions. The reason for standing on the thrower's side is that you assume his team will win the ball, and you will want to set your lines of sight and running so that, when it is won, you can follow play along the backs without having to run through a crowd of players. But you must be pragmatic about your positioning, not only because the ball is frequently won by the opposition. You may want to watch a particular player whom you suspect of infringement; you may have witnessed early domination by one side; and, most importantly, you must always stand on the goal-line side of a line-out when it is near to that goal-line. Why?

Firstly, you want to be ready for a participant to catch the ball and make a break for the goal-line, and you need to be in front of him to judge whether he grounds the ball for a try. Secondly, you are in a position which enables you to prevent offences by the defending side, such as offside by the backs. Thirdly, you can also spot infringements by the attacking team, such as the forward tap-through, where the jumper knocks the ball ahead of him for someone else to ground; the front peel, where a participant peels away and goes round illegally to the defending team's side of the line-out; and where the defending team's hooker is obstructed by the attacking player who has thrown in the ball.

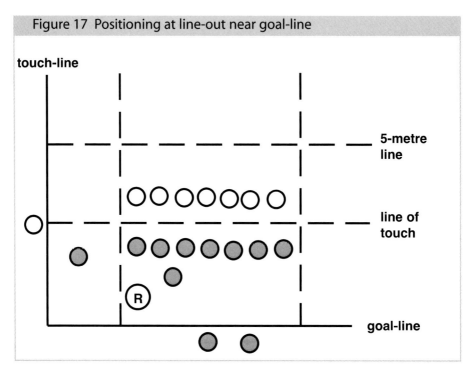

Figure 17 Positioning at line-out near goal-line

2.8 Line-out - referee's checklist

When the line-out is refereed well, the following elements will have been observed.

- Offences across the line-out are made a priority and are prevented and/or penalised.
- Offside by participants and non-participants is monitored.
- The ball is thrown in from the correct mark and along the line of touch.
- The quick throw-in is properly managed.
- The 1-metre gap is set and maintained.
- Lifting (as opposed to legal supporting) and illegal use of the outside arm are prevented.
- Participants remain within the 'corridor'.
- Preventive and punitive action is taken to achieve the above.
- The referee is always correctly positioned.

3 Penalty and free kicks, kick-offs and drop-outs

One of the early lessons you will learn as a referee is the phrase: 'Never stop refereeing'. What this means is that, even after a stoppage, you should still be on your toes and looking around you, as plenty of incidents occur when the ball is dead and all appears calm. This is especially true at situations when play is restarted by a kick.

3.1 Penalty and free kicks

For penalty and free kicks, the kicker's team have to behind the **ball** until it is kicked - most players think that they have to be behind the **kicker**, a misconception which is helpful to you as they tend not to infringe. The opponents must be 10 metres back from the mark (rather than the kicker, if he chooses to take the kick from behind the mark), and they are not allowed to enter the game until they have retired 10 metres, or until one of their team-mates who was 10 metres has run past and in front of them. At a free kick, opponents can charge as soon as the kicker begins his run or has offered to kick; if, in so doing, the opponents prevent the kick being taken, it is void and a scrum is awarded to the opposing team at the mark.

Figure 18   Positioning at penalty/free kick

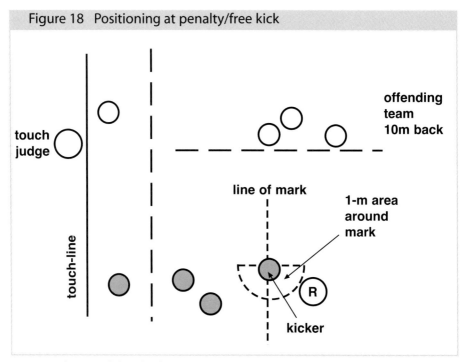

Tap penalties and free kicks can cause several problems for referees. You don't want to deny the kicking team an opportunity to gain an advantage so you must make the mark quickly and get away from it immediately so that they can take the kick in their own time, and you must give them some latitude as to exactly the spot from which they take it - a 1-metre area around the mark is reasonable. However, you have to be mindful of the fact that the kicker may be looking for an unfair advantage by taking the kick quickly and running direct-ly into opponents who have not retired. The opponents should not be penalised in this situation, but they must not interfere with play until they have retired the 10 metres or when one of their own players who was 10 metres back has passed them.

Some referees have decided to deal with this pragmatically, and will actually propose the following course of action to both skippers before kick-off: the ref-eree will give the kicking team the first 10 metres if opponents do not retire quickly enough, but he will be slower in making the mark for the next kick so as to give the opponents more time to retire. The Laws appear to support this, saying that a further penalty or free kick should not be awarded if the referee is satisfied that the reason for this has been contrived by the kicker's team.

If a team says that it intends to take a kick at goal, that intention is irrevo-cable and the kicker cannot then change his mind. However, if he places the ball for a kick at goal and it then falls over, he can pick it up and drop a goal.

For free kicks, and scrums taken in lieu of free kicks, remember that a dropped goal cannot be scored until after the ball next becomes dead, or the ball has been played or touched by an opponent, or an opponent has tackled the ball carrier, or a maul has formed.

Where you stand for a penalty or free kick depends on the circumstances, but is usually as indicated in **Figure 18**. Once you have made your mark, you must move off in a lateral direction as quickly as possible, watching the opponents to make sure they are 10 metres back or are making an effort to retire. You will know whether the kicker is going to go for touch, take a tap kick, go for goal, or put up a high ball, so move into a position from which you can clearly see the outcome as well as watching most of the players. Keep on your toes at all times, ready to follow up all kicks regardless of the anticipated outcome: many kicks don't reach touch, for instance, and you've got to be prepared for that.

3.2 Kick-offs

A kick-off occurs at the beginning of each half (when it must be a place kick) and after a score (when it must be a drop-kick). The kicker's team must be behind the ball **when kicked**: as with penalty and free kicks, most players don't realise this and think they have to be behind the kicker. The receiving team has to be on or behind their 10-metre line; if they aren't, the kick is taken again. A fair catch (mark) cannot be made directly from a kick-off. If the ball is kicked directly over the opposing team's goal-line, without touching or being touched by another player, and that team touches it down or makes it dead or it goes dead, they have the option of a scrummage at the centre of the half-way line or having the other team kick off again.

The referee needs to take up a position which enables him to watch the kicker's team as it moves up with the kicker, and to see the opposition (*see* **Figure 19**). He should be running as the kick is taken, but he must be careful to ensure that he does not get in the way if the kicker decides to change the angle of his kick. The referee also needs to be mindful of obstruction by the receivers: it's a common ploy for the catcher to be surrounded by team-mates, some or all of whom will form a wall in front of him, which makes them offside. Watch the catcher to make sure he isn't tackled in mid-air, which is dangerous play and should be severely dealt with.

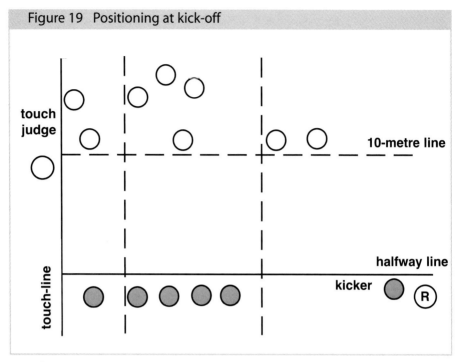

Figure 19 Positioning at kick-off

3.3 Drop-outs

Drop-outs are fairly straightforward, but there are a couple of problems of which you should be aware. The kicker's team has to be behind the ball when kicked; if not, a scrum is given to the non-offending team in the centre of the 22-metre line, but infringing players should not be penalised if their failure to retire is because of the speed with which the kick is taken. In these circumstances the offside players must not stop retiring and must not enter the game until they have been put onside by the action of their team-mates (*see* section 3.1 for details).

As long as the ball crosses the 22, play can continue, even if it is blown back or curls to such an extent that it comes back. Advantage can be played when the drop-kick does not reach the 22. If the attacking team makes the ball dead by a kick, other than an unsuccessful kick at goal, the defending team has the option of a drop-out or a scrum; if they choose the latter, it will be ordered at the place from where the ball was kicked. This Law is designed to discourage negative kicking tactics.

The referee should stand on or near the 22 for the kick, and should be positioned so that he can see the majority of the players, but he must not get in the way of the kicker if he changes the angle of the kick. The referee should be running as the kick is taken.

3.4 Restarts from kicks - referee's checklist

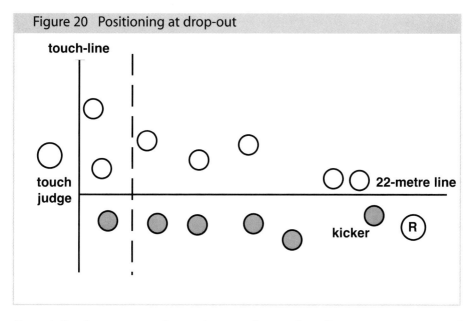

Figure 20   Positioning at drop-out

Essentially, there are two key points to observe for effective management of these restarts.

- Players must be behind the ball at kick-offs. They must be behind the ball at penalty and free kicks and drop-outs unless their failure to retire is due to the speed at which these kicks are taken and they must still conform to the offside Laws covering this situation.

- Management of penalty and free kicks - taken from correct place, referee moves away from mark quickly, kick correctly taken, 10 metres observed and enforced, ball made available by offending team.

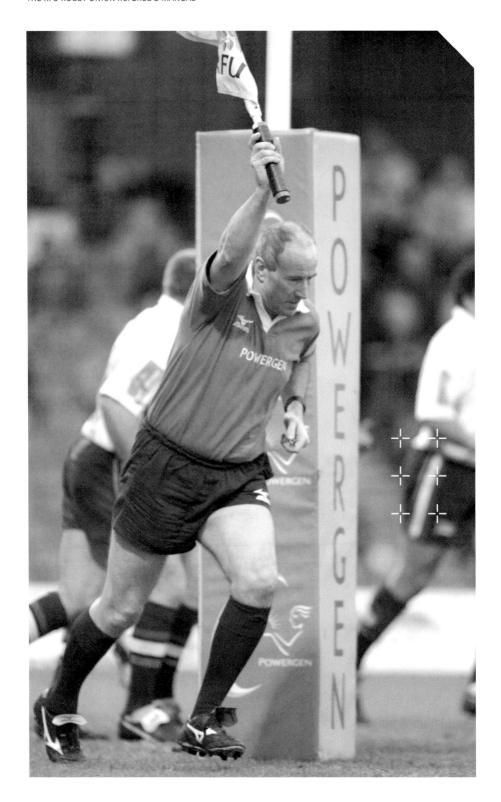

CHAPTER 5

Getting better

As with any role that involves a high degree of responsibility, the task of refereeing goes hand-in-hand with Training and Development. It is in everyone's interests that all referees, at whatever level they operate, are properly prepared and, from the moment you pick up the whistle, you will be supported with a wide variety of training courses and materials, as well as more informal development.

But that preparation is not a unilateral commitment. Successful referees are more than willing to participate in training and development programmes, and make a commitment to keep themselves informed about the game and the changing nature of the Laws and their interpretation. It is not sufficient simply to go on an introductory training course: Referee Development is a continuous process which never ends. As the game evolves, the Laws have to change to deal with new ways of playing, and referees need to know and understand how to adapt their management skills to handle new situations.

The Referee Society

The central point for most training and development is normally the Referee Society. These Societies are autonomous bodies, but part of the Rugby Football Referee's Union. They exist primarily to allocate referees to fixtures in their chosen geographic region: clubs in that region usually pay a membership fee to their local Society, in return for which they will receive referees for their matches. The Societies are largely dependent on their member clubs to provide a continuing supply of new referees because every season, a number of referees retire, move away or can no longer devote enough time. Societies and their member clubs work closely to recruit new referees so that matches at all levels can go ahead with a trained official. As these Societies have grown they have taken on a number of other functions, the most important of which is referee training.

Societies have appointed a Training Officer to handle this specific issue. There are basically two forms of training: formal programmes, developed centrally by the RFU, and less formal, but equally vital, meetings and discussion groups.

Basic training

Formal training is based on the core courses mini/midi (under-7 to under-12), and foundation for under-19 rugby. These award schemes are designed as a comprehensive introduction to refereeing, and many Societies promote them as the base level of training for new referees. The award programmes are not intended as a substitute for learning the Laws, but focus on interpretation and game management. Society Training Officers run the award schemes, which tend to be over a number of evenings and may culminate in a practical session where the attendees watch a match and comment on the referee's performance.

Not everybody, however, can make the necessary commitment to joining a Society and refereeing in various different locations every week. Recognising this, the RFU has courses for people who want to referee but would prefer to handle fixtures at their own club. There is an increasing recognition that clubs can no longer pull 'old Fred' out of the bar just before kick-off, give him a whistle and hope he can last for 80 minutes. Nowadays all matches, at whatever level, need to be managed by a qualified referee. Societies therefore encourage those who want to referee at their own club and support them with the relevant course. However, it should be stressed that a certificate is merely the start of the training process, and it must be supplemented with additional learning. Some Societies rightly suggest that participants in the mini/midi or foundation courses also join the local Referee Society so that they can benefit from ongoing training and development programmes and stay in touch with other referees.

Teachers should do the foundation course as it is vital that they are properly trained in the basic elements of refereeing. The Law variations for under-19 rugby put a heavy emphasis on safety, and the course reflects this. As with all other formal training programmes, this certificate provides a core of knowledge and understanding, but cannot be viewed as the complete training solution.

As you progress up the ladder, further training courses are available, where more emphasis is put on the finer points of refereeing - such as mental preparation, fitness, game preparation, and self-analysis. At the higher levels, referees are constantly monitored and are streamed according to competence and potential. Training and development is therefore a continuum, with performance benchmarks being raised as the referee progresses.

The Foundation Programme is the basic training for those joining a society. As referees move into the C grades there is a **National C Grade** programme which has to be completed before moving on to the **B Grade** programme. For all of these the RFU has produced Tutor Guides, presentation packages and participant materials.

If referees progress above the B grade level, they move into the elite **RFU Panel of National Referees**, where training and development is focused on personal development plans which analyse individual refereeing goals,

Personal Refereeing Development Plan

The purpose of this file is to provide you with an opportunity to generate your own refereeing development plan.

This should be seen as something to live with you so that you monitor your progress and review your plans accordingly.

You can use it as a basis for discussion with a referee coach or mentor. You can keep your assessment reports in it. It is yours to keep and use as you require.

Personal refereeing goals

Outline below your refereeing goals/ambitions
including target dates.

-
-
-
-
-

Strengths

Record below your refereeing strengths.

-
-
-
-
-

Weaknesses

Record below the areas of your refereeing requiring
further development.

-
-
-
-
-

Opportunities

What opportunities are there for you to build on your strengths and
develop the areas requiring attention?

-
-
-
-
-

Threats

What are the threats to you achieving your goals, i.e. what is hindering your progress?

-
-
-
-
-

Action planning

You

What actions can you take to build upon the opportunities and to minimise the threats?

-
-
-
-
-

Others

What practical actions can others take to help you to achieve your goals - who and what?

-
-
-
-

Mentor

Who are you going to discuss the personal refereeing plan with?

What qualifies them for the role of mentor:

- an "elder statesman"?
- another referee?
- a sports coach?

• a work place coach?
• a good listener?
• a confidant?
• a facilitator?

Clubs

Most clubs train and/or plan at the same mental or physical pace at least twice a week. If you were to make the next steps which clubs could you visit to ensure that you are operating at that same pace?

•

•

•

•

•

When will you start working with them?

strengths, weaknesses, opportunities for development and threats to that development. This analysis culminates in an action plan. A sample action plan is set out below: it's never too early to start!

Within the RFU Panel of National Referees there are regional squads and focus groups which meet for training and development sessions. Referees in the panel of National Referees will have coaches whose task is to maintain the referees' performance at peak levels and help these referees to resolve any problems they may have.

The Training and Development pyramid is shown in **Figure 21**.

Society training

Although the Referee Societies are run by unpaid volunteers, that does not mean that their approach to the job is anything less than professional. Societies provide referees to all levels of the game and must therefore ensure that the training they give is comprehensive and tailored to specific needs. Typically, a Society will run monthly meetings - open to all - which will include administrative items on the agenda but which will be largely devoted to aspects of the game. For instance, a schedule of meetings might cover Law changes, the scrum, onside/offside, communication, ruck and maul, the team of three and the line-out. These more informal sessions give the Societies and their mem-

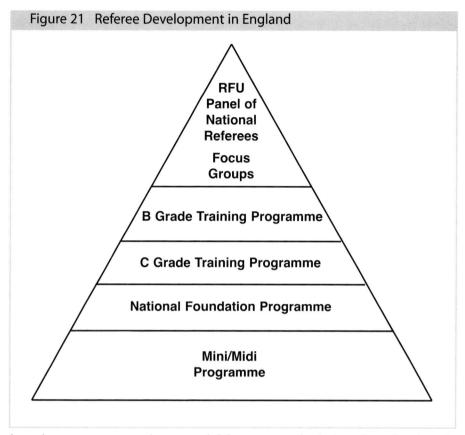

Figure 21   Referee Development in England

bers the opportunity to discuss and debate issues which directly and indirectly affect them in a relaxed and friendly forum.

Society meetings also give referees an opportunity to meet each other in a social setting. There is enormous benefit in being able to talk to other referees, finding out how they handle particular situations and sharing knowledge and experience. Especially for new referees, these meetings are an invaluable addition to the formal training programmes on offer.

Climbing the ladder

For the new referee, the development process begins with foundation training. For various reasons, some referees do not progress further, but there is no problem with this. They hone their skills working with children or the players at their own clubs. New Society referees are now expected to complete the National Foundation programme, early on in their career, at which point they are graded as a C3 referee. The grades are shown in **Figure 22**.

Figure 22 Referee's Grades

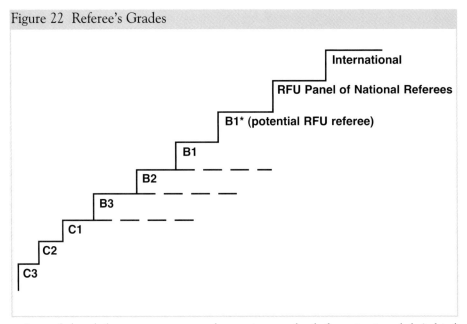

At each level the games start to change in standard, from junior clubs' third XVs to teams at level 5 in the leagues for B1 or B1* referees. The RFU Panel of National Referees rise to the dizzy heights of the Zurich Premiership.

How am I doing?

Refereeing involves a significant investment of time and effort, and no-one wants to see that investment wasted. For any referee to improve - and, as importantly, to feel that they are improving - there has to be a method of assessment in place which accurately and objectively measures performance and potential. Most referees are naturally self-critical animals, and are much more interested in what they're doing wrong than in what they're doing right. They appreciate informed opinion, advice and counsel so that they can better themselves, as well as managing and enjoying their games more. Remember that it is more important to be developed than promoted. Everyone can improve but not everyone can go up to the next grade.

Referee performance measurement, of course, can never be entirely scientific. Both the assessor and the assessed are only human, and no measurement system can legislate for personal foibles and idiosyncrasies. However, the RFU, the clubs and the Referee Societies have developed a number of different ways of looking at the performance of referees which, when taken as a whole, give an excellent indication of existing skills and weaknesses and areas for future development.

Club grading cards

Clubs have to be generally satisfied with the referees provided to them. This does not mean to say that referees set this as a top priority, but it is obviously important that the clubs value and respect the work done by referees and their Societies. Without that level of trust and confidence, the game would soon collapse. As a result, clubs are often asked to assess the performance of their referees for each fixture.

Most Societies provide referees or clubs with grading cards which are handed to both captains before the game. These cards ask the captains a variety of questions about the way in which the game was managed by the referee, and the captains are expected to give a mark for each element of competence. Individually the scores cannot be used as a completely valid method of assessment, but over the course of a season there will undoubtedly be discernible trends. No referee can hope for absolute consistency of grades, because the scores awarded by captains will vary according to their knowledge of the Laws, their position on the field, the result of the game and numerous other factors. However, club grading cards are very important for three reasons.

- They demonstrate to the clubs that the referee administrators are keen to improve the quality of refereeing, and value the opinion of the clubs they serve.

- They deliver important data on the players' perspective of a referee's performance

- They are the primary method of referee assessment at the lower end of the game.

Societies encourage clubs to fill in and return the cards as part of the post-match routine. The results are fed into a database which is then used as one element in the performance measurement process. Referees receive their individual results on a regular basis and can use these to concentrate on aspects of their performance which need further development.

The club cards are simply one strand in the assessment process, and no referee's career is dependent solely on the input of the clubs. The grades represent a trend, and a view from one constituency of the game. If weaknesses are highlighted by these grades, there are more formal and objective methods of remedial action.

The Competence-based Referee Development System

Whilst input from clubs is important, referees also need to be monitored more formally - and the best people to perform that task are other referees! Only when you have been a referee can you know how difficult and challenging the task can be, and you have a much greater empathy with the referee as a result.

The RFU has devised the Competence-based Referee Development System to inject higher levels of consistency into the process of performance measurement. The system is based on Units of Competence, which cover all the major elements of a game - Management of the Game, Management of Touch Judges, Scrum, Line-Out, Tackle, Ruck and Maul, Advantage, Open Play, Communication, Fitness, and Positioning. Each Unit of Competence is scored according to a pre-determined set of criteria.

Very good - to be awarded when all the elements of competence are covered consistently throughout the game.

Good - awarded when all the prioritised elements of competence are covered consistently throughout the game.

Minor development - awarded when, on most occasions, the prioritised elements of competence are adhered to.

Needs development - awarded when there is clear evidence he has knowledge of and has adhered to all elements of competence but has not applied them consistently throughout the game.

Significant development - awarded when the referee has demonstrated a knowledge of the elements of competence but has not adhered to them effectively nor consistently.

Additionally, the Adviser provides information on the referee's potential, indicating what needs to be done to fulfil that potential.

Referee Advisers, drawn from the ranks of existing and retired referees, use the system to assess the performance of referees and, more importantly, to provide feedback and advice to both the individual referee and his Society. A standard form is used by the Adviser (*see* pages 98-9), with copies being provided to the referee and his Society.

The Referee Adviser normally introduces himself to the referee well before the game and then gets out of his way! He observes the referee's pre-match preparations and the way in which he interacts with the players and club officials; he may, if invited, also attend the touch judge briefing from the referee (if touch judges have been appointed). One of the special skills of the Adviser is to understand that he is not there to watch the game: his sole interest is the referee's performance and his management skills. He will not make any comments at half-time or other breaks in play: this is important because the players get used to the particular style of the referee during the game and this should not be disrupted.

After the game, when the referee is showered and changed, the Adviser will give his feedback on the referee's performance. This is intended to be a constructive and informal session in which the Adviser gives praise where it is due and highlights the important areas that need attention. This session also gives the referee an opportunity to seek advice and clarification on any aspect of his match, so it should be a conversation rather than a lecture.

Once the report has been completed by the Adviser and received by the referee and his Society, it will form another part of the performance measurement analysis. Assessments by Advisers become more frequent if you move up the ladder and are handling fixtures, although most Societies aim to have all their referees assessed on a regular basis.

Coaching systems

Many societies and federations have developed coaching schemes for their referees.

There has been a variety of approaches to coaching, but most systems could be characterised as being :

(a) easier to produce, read and respond to

(b) more positive in their approach to development

(c) likely to make the referee want to turn out next week.

The coach can attend matches with his/her referee(s) and this continuity can help to build competence and confidence in the referee. The coach needs to know the referee will understand what makes him/her tick and be able to advise on off-the-field matters as well as on-the-field matters.

The mentor system

There are never enough Referee Advisers to cover as many fixtures as would be ideal, so some Referee Societies have introduced mentoring as a supple-

**RUGBY
FOOTBALL
UNION**

RFU REFEREE

REFEREE ASSESSMENT FORM 2

NAME OF REFEREE   LEVEL   SOCIETY

MATCH TYPE   LEVEL   DATE

MATCH RESULT

---

1. CHALLENGE OF THE MATCH:

---

2. MATCH MANAGEMENT:

PLEASE ASSESS THE REFEREE'S MATCH MANAGEMENT USING THE CRITERIA:

---

3. THE REFEREE'S POTENTIAL:

SIGNATURE OF ASSESSOR: DATE:

NAME: SOCIETY:

4.   KEY COMPONENTS

TACKLE   ADVANTAGE
RUCK   MAUL
KICKS   SCRUM
LINE-OUT

AREAS TO DEVELOP - Please select up to three of the above units to outline areas that need to be developed using the Key Components Descriptors.

Tackle
Scrum
Line Out

REFEREE'S STRENGTHS - Please select up to three of the above units to outline the referee's strengths in this match, using the Key Components descriptors.

Ruck / Maul
Advantage
Kicks

Please send one copy of this form direct to the Referee, and the Officers as directed by your Society, Federated Society or Group. This should normally be done within 48 hours of the match. Email is acceptable.

mentary method of helping referee development.

A mentor is someone who, through his experience, is in a position to help others develop their potential. Mentors do not usually attend matches as the Coach or Advisor would do.

This help comes in four ways:

- as an **adviser** to help clarify what needs to be achieved and possible routes for development
- as a **coach** to help develop a realistic view of skill levels and how to improve them
- as a **facilitator** to help identify or create appropriate opportunities for development
- as a **counsellor** to assist the referee in solving his own problems.

Particularly at the beginning of your career as a referee, you are likely to run into some problems, both in terms of your performance on the pitch and the administration and management of the match off the pitch. It isn't always easy to find the answers to all your questions, so some Societies have put a mentoring system in place so that referees have someone to whom they turn when they need information or clarification.

Although no two Societies operate the system in precisely the same way, the principles are fairly similar. Experienced referees act as mentors: they are likely to have a group of referees of different grades under their wing, some of whom will need more attention than others. Some referees decide that they don't need a mentor, whilst others use theirs frequently - there are no hard-and-fast rules, and mentoring is not obligatory.

The best mentors offer a sympathetic ear and give clear and practical guidance. They are trusted and treat all their relationships with confidentiality unless otherwise instructed. Where it is obvious that one of their referees needs help, they may come to a match to watch that referee or, with the referee's permission, send an Adviser. Their full value can only be realised if referees contribute to the relationship and listen to the advice the mentor gives them.

Effectively, the mentoring system gives referees access to the Society's pool of experience and knowledge through an informal medium, allowing referees to discuss their aspirations, problems and concerns with a wise and trusted counsel.

Society 'friends'/Club Advisers

As a further method of monitoring referee performance, some Societies have built a network of 'friends', people who will help the Society whenever they can and whose judgement is trusted and valued. Usually these friends are involved in the game as club coaches or administrators, and they will be standing on the touch-line during the match.

These people can give invaluable feedback to the Referee Society on the performance of their referees. They do not need to be trained Advisers, but they will still have an empathy for the match and they will instinctively know whether the referee is doing a good job and how he relates to the players. It's always useful to have another informed opinion on how a referee manages a match, especially when that opinion comes from someone who is not necessarily directly involved in refereeing. Their feedback and input can form another element in building an understanding of how referees perform, and many Societies are developing these contacts to add a further layer to their measurement and assessment routines.

The RFU has produced a training programme for Club Advisers – the Level 1 Adviser – which provides more details for clubs and potential Advisers; this can be obtained from your local Referee Society.

What next?

Having got this far, you find yourself still interested in becoming a referee. You don't yet know whether you'll be any good, but no-one does - it's only when you get out there with a whistle in your hand that you'll discover that! But what do you have to do now to get started?

You could conceivably begin by jumping in at the deep end and refereeing some matches at your local club. If you can get your hands on a current Law book, and you've had experience as a player, this is a possibility. However, many people nowadays prefer to do some basic referee training before they start: not only does this give you more confidence, but it also strengthens your position with regard to player safety and gives you the benefit of access to the Society's expertise and advice.

You will join the Society which covers the region in which you live. In some areas these Societies are grouped together with one Senior Society and a number of Associate Societies. In this case you would join an Associate Society and, if and when appropriate, you would move up to the Senior Society. Most Societies operate on a regional basis, so that you would not be expected to travel the length and breadth of the county or district each Saturday. However, the more senior you become, the more travelling will be expected of you, and you will find yourself on referee exchanges where you go to a completely different area under the control of another Society.

All the Referee Societies are listed in the Law book and the RFU Handbook (and a list of contacts is included in Appendix 2). You can also find out about the Societies by getting in touch with the RFU's Referee Department, and your local rugby club should have up-to-date details of whom to call. A lot of Societies have a dedicated Recruitment Officer who will give you all the information and encouragement you need.

One of the first questions you will be asked by a Society is about your availability: 'When do you want to start?'. Whatever you decide to do, you should not be put under any pressure to start until you are happy to do so. No-one wants to send out a referee who isn't fully prepared, as that is the quickest way to damage the referee's confidence - and the players won't be happy either. If you'd prefer to attend a Society meeting first, or go on a Foundation Programme, make this clear and it will be noted and understood. As far as is possible, the Society will try and accommodate your requirements, but do bear in mind that it cannot expend unlimited amounts of energy on you if you never go near a game. Set yourself a target date to begin refereeing, and stick to it.

You should also remember to be pragmatic and realistic about your availability. Naturally your Society will want you to be available as much as possible, but they would much prefer to know that you are reliable for two Saturdays every month than unreliable for all of them. Do not over-promise or over-commit, as this will inevitably cause problems at some stage. You are not expected to be available all the time, but you are expected to be available when you say you will be.

Mutual expectations

As a referee and a member of a Society, you will have certain expectations, which might include the following.

- Fixtures will be arranged for you by the Society.
- Clubs will treat you with respect and good manners.
- You will be kept informed of changes in Law and interpretation.
- You will be offered training and development programmes.
- Your performance will be regularly monitored and assessed and you will receive objective and constructive feedback.
- You will be promoted solely on the basis of merit and potential.
- When you have concerns or questions, they will be given a proper hearing.
- You will be fully supported by your Society in matters concerning player discipline.

These are reasonable expectations and Societies try to live up to them. Equally, however, a Referee Society will expect certain things from you.

- You will keep the Society informed about your availability and will give as much notice as possible if this changes.
- You will inform the Society about relevant changes in personal circumstances (e.g. house move, change of contact details, injuries).
- You will act as an ambassador for refereeing in general and your Society in particular.
- You will always maintain the highest standards before, during and after your games.
- You will make every effort to encourage new recruits.
- You will keep yourself informed about developments in the game and will attend Society meetings and training sessions whenever possible.
- You will reach and maintain an appropriate level of fitness.
- You will, where possible, volunteer to help the Society's administration.

Becoming a referee demands these commitments, however frequently you turn out for your Society. You should bear in mind that the majority of Societies are entirely dependent on the income they earn from club subscriptions and therefore work to a very tight budget. If they spend money on phone calls and letters chasing recalcitrant referees, there will be less to spend on the more critical aspects of administration. Furthermore, a Society's administrators normally have full-time jobs and may well be active referees themselves, so their time is precious and limited: you can help them to use that time most effectively if you are co-operative and reliable. The Society is there to help you - but you must also help yourself and them.

And finally...

The game of rugby football is truly democratic. It accommodates all sizes and abilities - male and female - and every player can find their own level. The same applies to refereeing: regardless of your ambitions, the game will offer you a place in which you can enjoy yourself whilst significantly enhancing the enjoyment of players.

But, at whatever level you operate, you must never lose sight of the fundamental objective of the referee: **to manage an environment in which two sides can play and enjoy a game of rugby football within the Laws of the game.** You achieve this by applying the three basic principles of **Safety, Equity** and **the Laws**. Do this, and your contribution to the game will be respected and valued.

You won't always get it right, and you won't always be thanked even when you do. However, you will find that the more you learn, and the more you practice, the greater will be your enjoyment. The referee is the 31st player on the field, and his or her afternoon is just as important as the other 30 players. If players don't train, and don't work at their skills, they will not get as much out of the game as they might, and exactly the same is true for referees. Picking up the whistle doesn't mean that you stop the process of training, development and improvement; it simply means that you transfer your efforts to a different, and in many ways more challenging, discipline.

But, as a referee, you are still part of the game. One of the great strengths of rugby football is that the vast majority of referees are ex-players who have an enduring empathy with the game and all its participants. Becoming a referee does not automatically excommunicate you from that constituency. There is no 'us' and 'them' mentality in rugby and, as a referee, you are still considered to be a key participant.

There is no doubt that refereeing can be a stressful and challenging occupation, but it is, like any other skill, one that can be mastered through hard work, application, preparation and plenty of physical and mental training. You will only know how rewarding it can be when you've had a good match and both skippers want to buy you a drink afterwards.

More than ever, today's game needs good, qualified referees at all levels. This manual should be used as an aide-memoir, to remind you of what's involved and what's required, and is intended to form the basis of your preparation. But there is no substitute for going out on to the pitch and trying it for yourself - in exactly the same way as every other referee, be they at international or 'Extra B' level, began their careers. One final thought to carry with you on to the field of play: no-one succeeds as a rugby referee unless they enjoy it. It's a useful thing to bear in mind as you're running backwards in freezing January rain trying to remember the intricacies of the offside Law!

Recruitment Freephone Number

For anyone interested in refereeing, a freephone telephone number has been set up by the RFU's Referee Centre of Excellence. For details of your local recruitment officer, call freephone **01902 380 280**.

Referee signals

The use of referee signals is recommended in order to help the referee communicate with players and spectators.

Penality kick

Shoulders parallel with touch-line. Arm angled up, pointing towards non-offending team.

Free kick

Shoulders parallel with touch-line. Arm bent square at elbow, upper arm pointing towards non-offending team.

Try and Penalty Try

Referee's back to dead ball line. Arm raised vertically.

Advantage

Arm outstretched, waist high, towards non-offending team, for a period of approximately five seconds.

Scrum awarded

Shoulders parallel with touch-line. Arm horizontal pointing towards team to throw in the ball.

Forming a scrum

Elbows bent, hands above head fingers touching.

Throw-forward/forward pass

Hands gesture as if passing an imaginary ball forward.

Knock-on

Arm out-stretched with open hand above head, and moves backwards and forwards.

Not releasing ball immediately in the tackle

Both hands are close to the chest, as if holding an imaginary ball.

Tackler not releasing tackled player

Arms brought together as if grasping a player and then opening as if releasing a player.

Tackler or tackled player not rolling away

A circular movement with the finger and arm moving away from the body.

Entering tackle from the wrong direction

Arm held horizontal then sweep of the arm in a semi-circle.

Intentionally falling over on a player

Curved arm makes gesture to imitate action of falling player. Signal is made in direction in which offending player fell.

Diving to ground near tackle

Straight arm gesture, pointing downwards to initiate diving action.

Unplayable ball at ruck or tackle

Shoulders parallel with the touch-line, arm horizontal pointing towards the team to throw in the ball, then towards the other team's goal-line whilst moving it backwards and forwards.

Unplayable ball in maul

Arm out to award scrummage to side not in possession at maul commencement. Other arm out then swing it across body with hand ending on opposite shoulder.

Joining a ruck or a maul in front of the back foot and from the side

The hand and arm are held horizontally moving sideways.

Intentionally collapsing ruck or maul

Both arms at shoulder height as if bound around opponent. Upper body is lowered and twisted as if pulling down opponent who is on top.

Prop pulling down opponent

Clenched fist, and arm bent. Gesture imitates pulling opponent down.

Prop pulling opponent on

Clenched fist, and arm straight, at shoulder height. Gesture imitates pulling opponent on.

Wheeling scrum more than 90 degrees

Rotating index finger, above the head.

Foot-up by front-row player

Foot raised, foot touched.

Throw-in at scrum not straight

Hands at knee level imitating action of throw-in not straight.

Failure to bind fully

One arm out-stretched as if binding. Other hand moves up and down arm to indicate the extent of a full bind.

Handling ball in ruck or scrum

Hand at ground level, making sweeping action as if handling the ball.

Throw-in at line-out not straight

Shoulders parallel with touch-line. Hand above head indicates the path of the ball, not straight.

Closing gaps in line-out

Both hands at eye level, pointing up, palms inward. Hands meet in squeezing action.

Barging in line-out

Arm horizontal, elbow pointing out. Arm and shoulder move outwards as if barging opponent.

Leaning on player in line-out

Arm horizontal, bent at elbow, palm down. Downward gesture.

Pushing opponent in line-out

Both hands at shoulder level, with palms outward, making pushing gesture.

Early lifting and lifting in line-out

Both fists clenched in front, at waist level, making lifting gesture.

Off-side at line-out

Hand and arm move horizontally across chest, towards offence.

Obstruction in general play

Arms crossed in front of chest at right angles to each other, like open scissors.

Off-side scrum, ruck and maul

Shoulders parallel with touchline. Arm hanging straight down, swings in arc along off-side line.

Off-side choice: penalty kick or scrum

One arm as for penalty kick. Other arm points to place where scrum may be taken instead of kick.

Off-side under 10-metre Law or not 10 metres at penalty and free kicks

Both hands held open above head.

High Tackle (foul play)

Hand moves horizontally in front of neck.

Stamping (foul play: illegal use of boot)

Stamping action or similar gesture to indicate the offence.

Punching (foul play)

Clenched fist punches open palm.

Dissent (disputing referee's decision)

Outstretched arm with hand opening and closing to imitate talking.

Award of drop-out on 22-metre line

Arm points to centre of 22-metre line.

Ball held up in-goal

Space between hands indicates that ball was not grounded.

115

Physiotherapist needed

One arm raised indicates physiotherapist is needed for injured player.

Doctor needed

Both arms raised above head indicates a doctor is needed for injured player.

Bleeding wound

Arms crossed above head indicates player has bleeding injury and may be temporarily replaced.

Timekeeper to stop and start watch

Arm held up in air and whistle blown when watch should be stopped or started.

Appendix 2   Federated Referee Societies

Telephone numbers – H: Home; B: Business; M: Mobile

RFU COMBINED SERVICES FEDERATED SOCIETY OF REFEREES

CHAIRMAN: Brig Roddy Porter MBE, Commander, 3 Infantry Brigade, Mahon Barracks, BFPO 809. Tel: 02838 360700/0701 (B). Fax: 02838 360701. Email: Through Hon Sec.
SECRETARY/DISCIPLINE: Lt. Col. Iain Clyde, SO1 OPS Sust, DG Log (Land), DLO Andover, Monxton Road, Andover, Hampshire, SP11 8HT. Tel: 01722 416651 (H), 01264 382314 (B), 07879 4981587 (M). Fax : 01264 383956. Email: james.clyde2@ntlworld.com/ iain.clyde904@mod.uk
CS ADMINISTRATOR/FINANCE: Roy McCombe, 11 Bervie Drive, Murieston, Livingston, West Lothian, EH54 9HA. Tel: 01506 420398 (H), 07764 430998 (M), 01506 409935 (B). Fax: 01506 409935. Email: roymccombe@btinternet.com/roy.mccombe@sru.org.uk
RFRU REP: Ch. Tech. Andy Watson, 54 (F) Sqn RAF Coltishall, Norwich, Norfolk, NR20 3TJ. Tel: 01362 695071 (H), 07768 864472 (M), 01603 267768 (B). Email: awatson@tesco.net
RRDO (CS): WO1 (ASM) John Voss, The King's Royal Hussars, Light Aid Detachment, Aliwal Barracks, Tidworth, Hampshire, SP9 7BB. Tel: 01980 842725 (H), 07712 762598 (M), 94342 2728 (B). Fax: 01980 603143. Email: john@vossjvf.freeserve.co.uk
CS RRT (NORTH): WOII Tony Merone, The Tyne Tees Regt, The Eden Armoury, St Andrews Road, Bishop Auckland, Co Durham, DL14 6RX. Tel: 01325 240489 (H), 07801 650039 (M), 01388 605214 (B). Fax: 01388 664639. Email: tony@merone18.freeserve.co.uk
CS RRT (SOUTH): Cdr Roger Baileff RN, SO1 Benefits Realisation, JPA, Bray House, Worthy Down, Winchester, SO21 2RG: Tel: 01243 431712 (H), 07793 884230 (M), 01962 887161 (B). Fax: 01962 887677: Email: roger.baileff@ntlworld.com
REFEREE COACHING CO-ORDINATOR: Capt (Retd) Stuart Gray-Cowan, SO3 G1/G4 Gen, HQ 15 (NE) Bde, Imphal Bks, Fulford Rd, York, YO10 4AU. Tel: 01759 301398 (H), 07774 419369 (M), 01904 662052 (B). Fax: 01904 662010. Email: stuart@londesborough.demon.co.uk
CSRR NEWSLETTER EDITOR: Capt. Peter Coe, QM (T), 33 Engr Regt (EOD), Carver Barracks, Wimbush, Saffron Waldron, Essex, CB10 2YG. Tel: 01799 529203 (H), 07855 789008 (M), 01223 203666 (B). Email: pete.coe@talk21.com
CS APPOINTMENTS SECRETARY: Wng Cdr Iain Martin, LARO 8, RAF Wyton, Huntingdon, PE28 2EA. Tel: 01480 446080 (B). Fax: 01480 446747. Email: iain.martin@laro.mod.uk

Member Societies

Army – 1947
CHAIRMAN: Brig Roddy Porter MBE, Commander, 3 Inf Bde, Mahon Barracks, BFPO 809. Tel: 02838 360700/0701. Email: Through Hon Sec.
SECRETARY: Lt. Col. Iain Clyde, SO1 Op Sust, ES (Land); DLO (Andover), Monxton Road, Andover, Hampshire, SP11 8HT. Tel: 01722 416651 (H), 01264 382314 (B), 07879 491587 (M). Fax: 01264 383956. Email: iain.clyde904@mod.uk
FINANCE: Capt Steve Penfold, TASC TFCS IPT, Wheatstone Building, Blandford Camp, Blandford, Dorset, DT11 8RH. Tel: 01258 485408 (B). Fax: 01258 485592. Email: tfcshan04-penfoldstevecaptTFCS@mod.uk
CHAIRMAN RESOURCES AND PLANS: Maj. A Dale, Box HO80, HQ DEME (A); Hazelbrouck Barracks, Reading, Berks, RG2 9NJ. Tel: 0118 976 0171 (H), 07810 693054 (M), 0118 976 3863 (B). Fax:

117

0118 976 0171 (H), 0118 976 388 (B). Email: alanvickydale@hotmail.com
TRAINING & DEVELOPMENT OFFICER/CHAIRMAN ARURS GRADING COMMITTEE: WO1 (ASM) John Voss, The King's Royal Hussars, Light Aid Detachment, Aliwal Barracks, Tidworth, Hampshire, SP9 7BB. Tel: 01980 842725 (H), 07712 762598 (M), 94342 2728 (B). Fax: 01980 603143. Email: john@vossjvf.freeserve.co.uk
REFEREE COACHING CO-ORDINATOR: Capt (Retd) Stuart Gray-Cowan, SO3 G1/G4 Gen, HQ 15 (NE) Bde, Imphal Bks, Fulford Rd, York, YO10 4AU. Tel: 01759 301398 (H), 07774 419369 (M), 01904 662052 (B). Fax: 01904 662010. Email: stuart@londesborough.demon.co.uk
APPOINTMENTS SECRETARY: As per Combined Services Federation

Royal Air Force – 1966

CHAIRMAN: Wg Cdr Iain Martin, LARO, H Block, RAF Wyton, Huntingdon, Cambs. Tel: 01480 52451 ext 6080 (B). Fax: 01480 446747
SECRETARY: Sqn Ldr Andy Rolfe, SO2 Sp Pers Pol, HQ STC, RAF High Wycombe, Buckinghamshire, HP14 4UE. Email: sec_rafrurs@hotmail.com
FINANCE: MACR Dougie Bruce, 51 Sqn, RAF Waddington, Lincoln, LN5 9NB. Tel: 01522 726187 (B)
T&D MANAGER/ASSESSMENT & GRADING: Sqn Ldr Steve Williams, SC1, Rm U106, Bennett Pavilion, RAF Wyton, Huntingdon, Cambridgeshire, PE28 2EA. Email: theoldgoat@skwilliams.fsnet.co.uk
B GRADE/C GRADE TRAINER/APPTS SECRETARY/DISCIPLINE: As CSRR
OTHER DEP SEC: Sqn Ldr Dave Mason, 18 Swift Close, Deeping St James, Lincs, PE6 8QH. Tel: 07795 523713 (M). Email: sec_rafrurs@hotmail.com

Royal Navy – 1928

CHAIRMAN: Lt CDR Roger Baileff RN, 115 New Brighton Road, Emsworth, Hampshire, PO10 7QS. Tel: 01243 431712 (H), 01962 887161 (B), 07793 884230 (M). Fax: 01962 887480. Email: rogerbaileff@aol.com
SECRETARY/PR/DISCIPLINE/RECRUITMENT & RETENTION: Tim Bailey, 10 Fernie Close, Hill Head, Fareham, Hants, PO14 3SQ. Tel: 01329 314785 (H), 07712 328513 (M). Email: tim.bailey2@ntl-world.com
FINANCE: Cdr Stew Kilby RN, Directing Staff, D Division, Advanced Command & Staff Course JSCSC, Farringdon Watchfield, Swindon, SN6 8TS. Tel: 01300 320027 (H), 07971 512874 (M). Email: stewart.kilby@virgin.net
TRAINING & DEVELOPMENT: Paul Burton, 49 Watersmeet, Fareham, PO16 0TG. Tel: 01329 827765 (H), 07967 750203 (M), 02392 765193 (B). Email: paul.rachel@virgin.net
B/C GRADE TRAINER: As for CS Trainer
NATIONAL FOUNDATION TRAINER: As for CS
APPTS SECRETARY (Weekends/Midweek/Re Appts): CS Appts Sec, according to the geographical area.

WEST MIDLANDS FEDERATION

CHAIRMAN: John Burgum, 19 Claines Road, Northfield, Birmingham, B31 2EE. Tel: 0121 475 6702 (H)
SECRETARY: Colin MacDonald, 10 Lewis Close, Lichfield, Staffs, WS14 9UE. Tel: 01543 257254 (H), 07932 859289 (M). Email: colinmmac@aol.com
FINANCE: Ian Morton, Frensham, Main Street, Lenchwick, Evesham, WR11 4TG. Tel: 01386 870566 (H), 07949 107422 (M)
T&D MANAGER: Peter Harvey, 9 Windsor Road, Pattingham, Wolverhampton, WV6 7DR. Tel: 01902 700070 (H). Email: harvey53@hotmail.com
APPTS SECRETARY: Roy Meller, 42 Knights Hill, Aldridge, Walsall, WS9 0TG. Tel: 01922 745654 (H), 07831 824427 (M), 0121 2122334 (B). Fax: 01922 745654
ASSESSMENT & GRADING (ALL REPORTS): Robert Edwards, 8 Ridgeway Close, Hyde Lea, Stafford, Staffs, ST18 9BE. Tel: 01785 242542 (H). Fax: 01922 720410. Email: redwards@hoslington.fsbusiness.co.uk
RFRU REPRESENTATIVE: Colin MacDonald, 10 Lewis Close, Lichfield, Staffs, WS14 9UE. Tel: 01543

257254 (H), 07932 859289 (M). Email: colinmmac@aol.com

Member Societies

Staffordshire – 1964

CHAIRMAN/SADO: Peter Harvey, 9 Windsor Road, Pattingham, Wolverhampton, West Midlands, WV6 7DR. Tel: 01902 700070 (H). Email: harvey53@hotmail.com

SECRETARY/RECRUITMENT: Derek Pemberton, Marcus House, Crestwood Rise, Rugeley, Staffs, WS15 2XZ. Tel: 01889 577666 (H & B), 07836 775748 (M). Fax: 01889 577666. Email: srusr@tiscali.co.uk

FINANCE: Ian Hunter, 21 Seven Way, Cressage, Shrewsbury, Shropshire, SY5 6DS. Tel: 01952 510818 (H), 07958 551429 (M). Email: ianhunter@boltblue.net

T&D MANAGER: Colin MacDonald, 10 Lewis Close, Lichfield, Staffs WS14 9UG. Tel: 01543 257254 (H). Email: colinmmac@aol.com

PR & SPONSORSHIP: Tony Morrish, 156 High Street, Shasetown, Burntwood, Staffordshire, WS7 8XG. Tel: 01543 304124 (H), 07989 559023 (M). Email: foundridge@btconnect.com

APPTS SECRETARY SATURDAYS: Steve Barr, 2 Barley Croft, Whittington, Staffordshire, WS14 9LY. Tel: 01543 432605 (H), 07932 791396 (M). Email: stevebarruk@yahoo.com

RE-APPTS SECRETARY SATURDAY: David Watt, 14 Bonnard Close, Meir Park, Stoke on Trent, Staffordshire, ST3 7QX. Tel: 01782 397292 (H), 07817 907541 (M). Email: daviddonnawatt@tinyworld.co.uk

DISCIPLINE/MEMBERSHIP SECRETARY/REPORT CARDS: Paul Daniels, 28 Golborn Avenue, Meir Heath, Stoke on Trent, Staffs, ST3 7LT. Tel: 01782 396738 (H). Email: p.daniels3@ntlworld.com

ASSESSMENT FORMS CO-ORDINATOR: Bob Edwards, 8 Ridgeway Close, Hyde Lea, Stafford, Staffs, ST18 9BE. Tel: 01785 242542 (H). Email: redwards@heslington.fsbusiness.co.uk

North Midlands – 1925

PRESIDENT: John Burgum, 19 Claines Road, Northfield, Birmingham B31 2EE. Tel: 0121 475 6702 (H)

CHAIRMAN: Roy Meller, 42 Knights Hill, Aldridge, Walsall WS9 0TG. Tel: 01922 745654 (H), 07831 824427 (M), 0121 2122334 (B). Fax: 01922 745654

ADMINISTRATOR/SECRETARY: Dave Lloyd Thomas, 35 Pritchard Drive, Stapleford, Notts, NG9 7GW. Tel: 01159 499954 (H), 04104 98588 (M). Fax: 01159 499954. Email: dlt@refereecoach.fsnet.co.uk

FINANCE: Ian Moreton, Frensham, Main Street, Lenchwick, Nr. Evesham, Worcestershire WR11 4TG. Tel: 01386 870566 (H), 07949 107422 (M), 01905 722800 (B). Email: finance@nmsrfr.com

RECRUITMENT & RETENTION/NATIONAL FOUNDATION TRAINER: Alan Hughes, 18 Cedar Avenue, Bramford Estate, Bilston, Wolverhampton, WV14 9TN. Tel: 01902 882545 (H). Fax: 01902 676009. Email: cb-yregistrar-northmids@therfu.com

TRAINING & DEVELOPMENT: Ray Jones, 23 Blounts Road, Erdington, Birmingham, B23 7DA. Tel: 0121 382 0310 (H). Email: rayjones@aol.com

MARKETING: Peter Evans, 36 Balmoral Street, Kidderminster, Worcs DY10 3AH. Tel: 07768 405539 (M), 01562 515183 (B). Email: marketing@nmsrfr.com

APPTS SECRETARY WEEKENDS/RE-APPTS SATURDAY: Mike Spencer, 20 Wyckham Close, Harborne, Birmingham, B17 0TB. Tel: 0121 680 3415 (H), 0121 694 5006 (B). Fax: 0121 680 3415. Email: appointments@nmsrfr.com

APPTS SECRETARY MIDWEEK: Paul Rogers, Streamside, 14 High Street, Marton, Nr Rugby, CV23 9RR. Tel: 01926 633504 (H). Email: paul@rogers7100.freeserve.co.uk

RE-APPTS SECRETARY SUNDAY: Mick Fielding, 96 Vera Road, Yardley, Birmingham, B26 1TT. Tel: 0121 628 7852 (H), 07748 402443 (M), 0121 707 7111 x 5438 (B). Fax: 0121 628 7852. Email: keith.fielding@trw.com

DISCIPLINE: Peter Jordan, 25 Station Road, West Hagley, DY9 0NX. Tel: 01562 882176 (H)

ASSESSMENT & GRADING/SADO: Steve Hindson, 9 Coleford Close, Redditch, Worcs, B97 5UX. Tel: 01527 404248 (H), 0121 700 6650 (B). Fax: 0121 700 6650. Email: steve.hindson@lloydstsbautolease.co.uk

CENTRAL FEDERATION

CHAIRMAN: Dave Drabwell, 4 Lawrence Gardens, Kenilworth, Warwickshire, CV8 2GH. Tel: 01926 851087 (H), 01926 779923 (B), 07771 531690 (M). Email: dave.drabwell@ntlworld.com
SECRETARY: Ed Bawden, 13 Hampton Close, Bragbury End, Stevenage, Hertfordshire, SG2 8SP. Tel: 01438 811625 (H), 01438 755860 (B), 07855 928845 (M). Email: Ed.bawden@ukonline.co.uk
TREASURER: Stephen Oliver, 41 Sellars Grange, Orton Goldhay, Peterborough, PE2 5XX. Tel: 01733 235048 (H), 01354 657650 (B), 07771 545496 (M). Email: stephenoliver2@aol.com
FEDERATION REPRESENTATIVE TO RFRU/FADO: Brian Abrahams, 103 The Drive, Kingsley, Northampton, NN1 4SW. Tel: 01604 458353 (H), 07719 571081 (M). Email: b.abrahams@ntlworld.com
COACH DEVELOPMENT: Ian Baggott, 34 Cotswold Drive, Wellingborough, Northampton, NN8 2JB. Tel: 01933 270380 (H). Email: ianb@mem-recruitment.demon.co.uk
TRAINING & DEVELOPMENT: John Wearing, 145 Obleisk Rise, Kingsthorpe, Northampton, NN2 8TX. Tel: 01604 844882 (H). Email: john.wearing@ntlworld.com

Member Societies

Cambridge University & District – 1950
PRESIDENT: Mike Daniel, The New Barn, High Ditch Road, Fen Ditton, Cambridge, CB5 8TE. Tel: 01223 294317 (H)
CHAIRMAN: Ray Olds, 26 Abbey Street, Ickleton, Saffron Walden, Essex, CB10 1SS. Tel: 01799 530346 (H), 07702 237579 (M), 01223 423722 (B). Email: ray.olds@cosl.co.uk
SECRETARY: John Hooper, 11 Victoria Park, Cambridge, CB4 3EJ. Tel: 01223 474891 (H). Email: john.hooper3@ntlworld.com
FINANCE MANAGER: ICharles Osbourn, 24 Gunson Gate, Chelmsford, Essex, CM2 9NZ. Tel: 01245 250031 (H), 07789 107643 (M), 01277 367018 (B). Email: cosbourn@tinyonline.co.uk
RECRUITMENT & PUBLICITY: Matthew Lawrance, 10 Clay Pit Piece, Saffron Walden, Essex, CB11 4DR. Tel: 01799 501591 (H), 07866 507804 (M), 01223 374271 (B)
CHILD PROTECTION OFFICER: Tony Kennedy, 24 High Street, Grantchester, Cambridge, CB3 9NF. Tel: 01223 841258 (H), 07764 162859 (M), 01223 358966 (B). Email: a.j.kennedy@tinyworld.co.uk
T&D MANAGER/APPTS (LOCAL CLUBS): Ray Olds, 26 Abbey Street, Ickleton, Saffron Walden, Essex, CB10 1SS. Tel: 01799 530346 (H), 07702 237579 (M), 01223 423722 (B)
REFEREE DEVELOPMENT/APPTS (LOCAL CLUBS): Mike Runswick, 3 Thrifts Walk, Chesterton, Cambridge, CB4 1NR. Tel: 01223 356239 (H), 01223 252827 (B). Email: runs@mrc-dunn.cam.ac.uk
ASSESSMENT & GRADINGS MANAGER/APPTS (LOCAL CLUBS): Nick Pett, 29 Priams Way, Stapleford, Cambridge, CB2 5DT. Email: npa.cantab@ntlworld.com
NATIONAL FOUNDATION TRAINER: Tim O'Connell, 87 The Doles, Over, Cambridge, CB4 5QD. Tel: 07940 838670 (M)
APPOINTMENTS SECRETARY (UNIVERSITY AND COLLEGES): Glynn James, 31 Melbourne Road, Stamford, Lincs, PE9 1UD. Tel: 01780 756034 (H), 07960 296537 (M). Email: rgjames@waitrose.com
APPOINTMENTS SECRETARY (SCHOOLS): Ian Reid, 34 Greystoke Road, Cherry Hinton, Cambridge, CB3 9NF. Tel: 01223 562013 (H), 01223 247251 ext 1405 (B). Email: ian.reid620@ntlworld.com
RFU LAWS LABORATORY: Mike Dimambro, 1 Coles Road, Milton, Cambridge, CB4 6BL. Tel: 01223 473796 (H). Email: cudrrs.dimambro@ntlworld.com
DISCIPLINE: Tony Kennedy, 24 High Street, Grantchester, Cambridge, CB3 9NF. Tel: 01223 841258 (H), 01223 497611 (B). Email: a.j.kennedy@tinyworld.co.uk

East Midlands – 1925
PRESIDENT/DISCIPLINE (REFEREE SOCIETY): Colin Wright, 31 Fairmead Rise, Welford Road, Northampton, NN2 8PP. Tel: 01604 844766 (H), 07814 556181 (M). Fax: 01604 844766. Email: president@emrurs.org.uk

CHAIRMAN/RETENTION OFFICER: Dr. Paul Dunnett, 22 Miller Road, Bedford, MK42 9NZ. Tel: 01234 308885 (H), 07770 687455 (M), 01767 602417 (B). Email: chairman@emrurs.org.uk

SECRETARY/ASSESSMENT & GRADING (ALL REPORTS): Dr. Chris Rowan, 17 Blethan Drive, Stukeley Meadows, Huntingdon, Cambs, PE29 6GN. Tel: 01480 434959 (H), 07808 184274 (M), 01480 892838 (B). Fax: 01480 383121. Email: gensec@emrurs.org.uk

FINANCE: Stephen Oliver, 27 Monson Way, Oundle, Northants, PE8 4QG. Tel: 01832 273367 (H), 07715 545496 (M). Email: treasurer@emrurs.org.uk

APPOINTMENTS & GRADING CHAIRMAN: John Wearing, 145 Obelisk Rise, Kingsthorpe, Northampton, NN2 8TX. Tel: 01604 844882 (H), 07736 046059 (M), 01604 889010 (B). Fax: 01604 889095. Email: apptsgradingchair@emrurs.org.uk/johnwearing@btconnect.com

PR/RE-APPOINTMENTS SECRETARY: Clive Leeke, 298 Billing Road East, Northampton, NN3 3LJ. Tel: 01604 620941 (H), 07763 468851 (M). Fax: 01604 620941. Email: traindevchair@emrurs.org.uk

DEVELOPMENT REFEREE COURSE TRAINER: As Central Federation Training Officer

APPTS MANAGER (ALL EXCHANGES): Paul Rogers, 'Streamside', 14 High Street, Marton, Rugby, Warwickshire, CV23 9RR. Tel: 01926 633504 (H), 07952 856099 (M). Fax: 01926 633504. Email: apptsexchsec@emrurs.org.uk

APPTS SECRETARY (WEEKENDS): Martin Ellis, 144 Westbury Lane, Newport Pagnell, Bucks, MK16 8PT. Tel: 01908 614952 (H), 07763 466207 (M), 0207 170 7007 (B). Email: martin.ellis@thecarbontrust.co.uk

APPTS SECRETARY (MIDWEEK): Laurie Pearson, 'Avalon', Church Hill, Ravensthorpe, Northants, NN6 8EF. Tel: 01604 770750 (H), 07966 115504 (M), 01604 830381 (B). Fax: 01604 831865. Email: midwkapptssec@emrurs.org.uk

DISCIPLINE (CONSTITUENT BODY): Tony Mills, 1 Newbury House, Kimbolton Road, Bedford, MK40 2PD. Tel: 01234 212524 (H), 01234 347980 (B). Email: cb-honsec-eastmids@therfu.com

SADO: Kneale Grainger, 26 Lumbertubs Lane, Northampton NN3 6AH. Tel: 01604 462744 (H), 07788 842363 (M), 01604 641600 (B). Email: ruth.granger@virgin.net

Warwickshire – 1896

PRESIDENT: Gordon Miles, 8 Stivichall Croft, Coventry, CV3 6GN. Tel: 02476 414805 (H)

CHAIRMAN: Gwyn Airdrie, 32 Windsor Close, Tamworth, Staffordshire, B79 8UH. Tel: 01827 311825 (H). Email: gwynairdrie@ge.com

VICE CHAIRMAN/RECRUITMENT & DEVELOPMENT: Steve Davies, 2 Gratton Court, Green Lane, Coventry, CV3 6RD. Tel: 02476 416709 (H). Email: davies@9roman.freeserve.co.uk

HONORARY SECRETARY: Malcolm Murphy, 301 Smorrall Lane, Bedworth, Warwickshire, CV12 0LQ. Tel: 02476 364345 (H). Email: murphy_25551@btinternet.com

HONORARY TREASURER: Nick Edwards, 86 Shipston Road, Stratford on Avon, CV37 7LR. Tel: 01789 292869 (H), 07792 503144 (M). Email: nedwards1@tinyworld.co.uk

SOCIAL, MARKETING & SPONSORSHIP: Duccio Baldi, 22 Hawkshead Drive, Knowle, Solihull, B93 9QE. Tel: 01564 779826 (H), 07889 422627 (M). Email: duccio.baldi@accantia.com

CHAIR OF GRADING/ADVISER APPOINTMENTS SECRETARY: John Hall, 49 Middleborough Road, Coundon, Coventry, CV1 4DG. Tel: 02476 261640 (H). Email: john.hall16@ntlworld.com

SADO: Steve Latham, 20 Heather Drive, Bedworth, Warwickshire, CV12 0AT. Tel: 02476 317775 (H). Email: steve.latham@tesco.net

CLUB & DISTRICT LIAISON OFFICER: John Davies, Darlingscott, The Green, Long Itchington, Warwickshire, CV23 8PH. Tel: 01926 812013 (H)

KIT MANAGER: John Morton, 63 Shirley Road, Walsgrave, Coventry, CV2 2EL. Tel: 02476 617128 (H)

WARWICKSHIRE RFC REP: Richard Wormell, The Malt Shovel, Lower End, Bubbenhall, Coventry, CV8 3BW. Tel: 02476 303235 (H), 07810 200611 (M). Email: r.wormell@btopenworld.com

FEDERATION BOARD MEMBER: Dave Drabwell, 4 Lawrence Gardens, Kenilworth CV8 2GH. Tel: 01926 851087 (H). Email: dave.drabwell@ntlworld.com

APPOINTMENTS SECRETARY: TBA

EXCHANGE SECRETARY (SUNDAY & MIDWEEK): Dave Smith, 60 Deansway, Ash Green, Coventry, CV7 9HF. Tel: 07855 795380 (M). Email: smudgerref@aol.com

NATIONAL FOUNDATION COURSE TRAINER: Peter Tolan, 61 Pheasant Oak, Nailcote Grange, Coventry, CV4 9XJ. Tel: 024 7646 7231 (H), 07980 512231 (M)

SATURDAY RE-APPOINTMENTS SECRETARY: TBA
MIDWEEK RE-APPOINTMENTS SECRETARY: Deane Randall. Tel: 07930 834705 (M)
SUNDAY RE-APPOINTMENTS SECRETARY: Luke Haskins. Tel: 07743 306884 (M)

East Midlands – 1925

PRESIDENT: Brent May, 8 Lilac Way, Harpenden, Hertfordshire, AL5 1SQ. Tel: 01582 761703 (H), 07768 633718 (M), 01908 249476 (B). Email: president@hertsrefs.org

SECRETARY: Timothy Clarke, Rectory Farm House, Barton Road, Lower Gravenhurst, Bedfordshire, MK45 4JR. Tel: 01462 712628 (H), 07789 268873 (M). Email: secretary@hertsrefs.org

FINANCE: Brent May, 8 Lilac Way, Harpenden, Hertfordshire, AL5 1SQ. Tel: 01582 761703 (H), 07768 633718 (M), 01908 249476 (B). Email: treasurer@hertsref.org

RECRUITMENT: Keith Hurley, 139 Gordon Hill, Enfield, Middlesex, EN2 0QT. Tel: 0208 351 0108 (H), 07952 555837 (M). Email: membership@hertsrefs.org

PR/SPONSORSHIP & KIT: Peter Smith, 231 Cassiobury Drive, Watford, Hertfordshire, WD1 3AN. Tel: 01923 234258 (H), 07710 789185 (M). Email: pr@hertsrefs.org

T&D MANAGER/APPTS SEC. SATURDAYS: Ed Bawden, 13 Hampton Close, Stevenage, Hertfordshire, SG2 8SP. Tel: 01438 811625 (H), 07855 928845 (M), 01438 755860 (B). Email: training@hertsrefs.org

B GRADE TRAINER: Mark Abbas, 5A Barton Road, Upper Gravenhurst, Bedfordshire, MK45 4JP. Tel: 01462 712531 (H), 07970 284036 (M). Email: markabbas@aol.com

NAT FOUND/MINI MIDI TRAINER: Bill Ractliffe, 17 Lancaster Road, St. Albans, Hertfordshire, AL1 4EP. Tel: 01727 766987 (H), 07710 058187 (M). Email: bill.ractliffe@ual.com

APPTS SECRETARY (MIDWEEK), SUNDAYS: David Worker, 16 Cubbington Close, Luton, LU3 3XJ. Tel: 01582 576788 (H), 07951 157339 (M)

RE-APPTS SECRETARY: Roger Johns, 55 Old Park View, Enfield, Middlesex, EN2 7EQ. Tel: 0208 245 4096 (H)

DISCIPLINE: Philip Davies, 10 Danesbury Park, Bengeo, Hertfordshire, SG14 3HX. Tel: 07939 542339 (M). Email: discipline@hertsrefs.org

ASSESSMENT & GRADING: Mike Burdett, 78 Elmwood Crescent, Flitwick, Beds, MK45 1LJ. Tel: 01525 721157 (H). Email: assess@hertsrefs.org

SADO: Peter Jennings, Sunnymead, Barkway Road, Royston, Hertfordshire, SG8 9NB. Tel: 01763 245291 (H), 07781 627115 (M). Email: sado@hertsrefs.org

THE FOUR COUNTIES FEDERATION

CHAIRMAN: Trevor Sharpe, 8 Wheatfield Way, Ashgate, Chesterfield, Derbyshire, S42 7PB. Tel: 01246 550874 (H). Email: trevorsharpe@tiscali.co.uk

SECRETARY/NAT. FOUND & MM TRAINER: Brian Parkinson, 58 Redland Drive, Chilwell, Beeston, Nottingham, NG9 5LE. Tel: 0115 925 4250 (H), 07977 265670 (M), 0115 925 4250 (B). Fax: 0115 925 4250. Email: brianparkinson@rfu.com/bparki@chilwell58.freeserve.co.uk

FINANCE: TBA

T & D MANAGER/PR/ASSESSMENT & GRADING: Kerrel Wills, 10 Brook House Close, Rearsby, Leicestershire, LE7 4YG. Tel: 01664 424826 (H). Email: kerrel.wills@nottinghameveningpost.co.uk

COUNTY REP ON FED: Steve Bradford, 9 Elm Avenue, Long Eaton, Nottingham, NG10 4LR. Tel: 0115 913 2191 (H), 07710 646251 (M), 0115 969 1300 x 30175 (B). Email: steve.bradford@nottshc.nhs.uk

John Edwards, 40 Garden Street, Eastwood, Nottingham, NG16 3FW. Tel: 01773 770283 (H), 07787 158496 (M)

John Haggart, 64 Tennyson Road, Lutterworth, Leicestershire, LE17 4XA. Tel: 01455 553167 (H), 07876 446599 (M), 01788 532359 (B). Email: John@rapak.com

APPTS SECRETARY MIDWEEK & WEEKENDS, SOCIETY OFFICER. FADO: TBA

Member Societies

Leicestershire – 1897

CHAIRMAN/APPTS SECRETARY (WEEKENDS): Nick Lacey, 1 Wentworth Close, Kibworth, Leicestershire, LE8 0XB. Tel: 0116 279 3605 (H), 07973 849490 (M). Email: nickl_kibworth@hotmail.com

SECRETARY/RECRUITMENT: Ian Roberts, 16 Chapel Close, Houghton on the Hill, Leicestershire, LE7 9HT. Tel: 0116 243 2228 (H), 07990 506822 (M), 0116 243 2818 (B). Fax: 0116 243 3753. Email: ian.roberts@contifibre.com

FINANCE: Don Hope, 12 Gynsill Lane, Anstey, Leicester, LE7 7AG. Tel: 0116 287 3783 (H). Email: donandjoanh@yahoo.co.uk

PR/RE-APPOINTMENTS SEC: Kerrel Wills, 10 Brook House Close, Rearsby, Leicestershire, LE7 4YG. Tel: 01664 424826 (H), 07971 539578 (M), 0115 948 2000 (B). Fax: 01664 424826. Email: kerrel.wills@nottinghameveningpost.co.uk

T&D MANAGER: Mike Mortimer, 34 Warwick Road, Littlethorpe, Leicestershire, LE9 5JA. Tel: 0116 286 6201 (H), 07970 782703 (M), 0116 286 6201 (B). Email: mike.mortimer@lineone.net

MINI/MIDI/NATIONAL FOUNDATION TRAINER: Malcolm Eames, 28 Hammond Way, Market Harborough, Leicestershire, LE16 7JP. Tel: 01858 466963 (H), 07890 929311 (M). Email: Malcolm.eames@virgin.net

APPTS SECRETARY (MIDWEEK/SATURDAY): Mark Elliott, 7 Tynedale Road, Loughborough, Leicestershire, LE11 3TA. Tel: 01509 557863 (H), 07960 495766 (M). Email: ark.elliott5@ntlworld.com

APPTS SECRETARY (SUNDAY): Stephen Gammage, 12 Orkney Close, Hinckley. Leicestershire, LE10 0TA. Tel: 01455 450403 (H), 07732 667732 (M). Email: Stephen.gammage@btopenworld.com

ASSESSMENT & GRADING: Dennis Belton, 20 Church Hill, Woodhouse Eaves, Loughborough, Leicestershire, LE12 8RT. Tel: 01509 890824 (H). Fax: 01509 890824. Email: lsrur.laptop@tiscali.co.uk

SADO: John Haggart, 64 Tennyson Road, Lutterworth, Leicestershire, LE17 4XA. Tel: 01455 553167 (H), 07876 446599 (M), 01788 532359 (B). Email : johnh@rapak.com

Notts, Lincs & Derby – 1933

PRESIDENT: Stephen Tinkler, 14 High Street, South Anston, Sheffield, S31 7AY. Tel: 01909 563288 (H). Email: stevetinkler@eeingleton.co.uk/president@nldrfusr.co.uk

CHAIRMAN: Trevor Sharpe, 8 Wheatfield Way, Ashgate, Chesterfield, Derbyshire, S42 7BP. Tel: 01246 207647 (H), 07974 761286 (M). Email: trevsharpe@tiscali.co.uk/ chairman@nldrfusr.co.uk

SECRETARY: Mark Camm, 94 Ruskin Avenue, Lincoln, Lincolnshire, LN2 4BT. Tel: 01522 519261 (Rugby line), 07947 139215 (M). Email: markcamm.rugby@btopenworld.com/secretary@nldrfusr.co.uk

FINANCE: John Edwards, 40 Garden Road, Eastwood, Nottingham, NG16 3FW. Tel: 01773 770283 (H), 07787 158496 (M). Email: treasurer@nldrfusr.co.uk

RECRUITMENT & RETENTION: Tim Murrie, 28 Mosgrove Close, Gateford Meadows, Worksop, Notts, S81 8TD. Tel: 07971 781574 (M). Email: climbingmoncrief@aol.com

PR/WEBMASTER: Paul Carroll, 104 Station Road, Stanley, Derbyshire, DE7 8FB. Tel: 0115 944 4042 (H), 07711 860169 (M). Email: pc@subantartic.org.uk/webmaster@nldrfusr.co.uk

TRAINING & DEVELOPMENT MANAGER/ ASSESSMENT & GRADING: Steve Bradford, 9 Elm Avenue, Long Eaton, Nottingham, NG10 4LR. Tel: 0115 913 2191 (H). Email: steve.bradford@nottshc.nhs.uk/training@nldrfusr.co.uk

NATIONAL FOUNDATION TRAINER/SADO: Brian Parkinson, 58 Redland Drive, Chilwell, Beeston, Nottingham, NG9 5LE. Tel: 0115 9254250 (H). Fax: 0115 9254250. Email: brianparkinson@rfu.com /sado@nldrfusr.co.uk

APPOINTMENTS/RE-APPTS/MIDWEEK: Trevor Sharpe, 8 Wheatfield Way, Ashe, Chesterfield, Derbyshire, S 7PB: Tel: 01246 7647 (H), 07974 61286 (M). Email: trevorsharpe@tiscali.co.uk/fixtures@nldrfusr.co.k

DISCIPLINE: Andre Russell, 1 High Street, Messingham, Nr Scunthorpe, North Lincs, DN17 3UD. Tel: 01724 764696 (H). Fax: 01724 764696. Email: andrerussell1965@aol.com

FEDERATION OF RUGBY UNION REFEREES SOCIETIES OF THE NORTH

CHAIRMAN: Malcolm Shorney, 5 The Paddock, Middleton St. George, Darlington, DL2 1BT. Tel: 01325 332773 (H). Email: malcolm.shorney@virgin.net/malcolmshorney@rfu.com
SECRETARY: Peter Howe, 6 Burnland Terrace, Hexham, Northumberland, NE46 3JT. Tel: 01434 606533 (H), 01670 534082 (B), 07802 433149 (M). Email: phexchanges@yahoo.co.uk
TREASURER: Geoff Parkinson, 16 Sturdee Gardens, Jesmond, Newcastle upon Tyne, NE2 3QT. Tel: 0191 2859431 (H). Email: geoff@parki1.fsnet.co.uk
RFRU REPRESENTATIVE: Jim Coulson, Shotley Cottage, 28 Snows Green, Shotley Bridge, Consett, DH8 0HA. Tel: 01207 503022 (H), 07785 398496 (M), 01207 580312 (B). Fax: 01207 580383. Email: jim.coulson@btinternet.com
CHAIR APPOINTMENTS WORKING PARTY: Mike Firby, 4 Clifton Gardens, Great Clifton, Workington, CA14 1TT. Tel: 01900 605631 (H), 01900 68141 (B). Fax: 01900 65075. Email: mf@firpressaccounts.ndo.co.uk
CHAIR RPSC & CHAIR ADVISERS WORKING PARTY: Bob Ward, 79 Grange Road, Morpeth, Northumberland, NE61 2UE. Tel: 01670 503991 (H), 07788 566479 (M), 01670 503015 (B). Fax: 01670 504188
SECRETARY RPC: Alan Jenkinson, 18 Station Road, Workington, CA14 2UZ. Tel: 01900 68960 (H), 01900 733366 (B). Email: alan.jenkinson@lsc.gov.uk
CHAIR TRAINING & DEVELOPMENT WORKING PARTY: John Richardson, The Vicarage, Whickham Bank, Swalwell, Newcastle, NE16 3LJ. Tel: 0191 488 1228 (H), 07775 514609 (M). Fax: 0191 489 8520 (B). Email: johnrichardson38@hotmail.com

Member Societies

Durham – 1895
CHAIRMAN/RRT NORTH: Malcolm Shorney, 5 The Paddock, Middleton St. George, Darlington, DL2 1BT. Tel: 01325 332773 (H). Email: malcolm.shorney@virgin.net
SECRETARY: John Denham, 84 Washington Crescent, Newton Aycliffe, County Durham, DL5 4AZ. Tel: 01325 304320 (H), 07800 962341 (M). Fax: 01325 304320. Email: johns.denham@virgin.net
FINANCE/EXCHANGES: David Sawyer, 78 Ark Royal Close, Warrior Park, Seaton Carew, Hartlepool, TS25 1DH. Tel: 01429 266799 (H), 07811 264585 (M). Email: davidcsawyer@btopenworld.com
T&D MANAGER: John Richardson, 'The Vicarage', Whickham Bank, Swalwell, Gateshead, NE16 3LJ. Tel: 0191 488 1228 (H), 07803 233090 (M). Email: johnrichardson38@hotmail.com
APPTS SECRETARY: Alan Thompson, 49 Carrsyde Close, Fellside Park, Whickham, Newcastle Upon Tyne, NE16 5UA. Tel: 0191 488 9672 (H). Email: alanthompson@durhamrefsoc.co.uk
RE-APPTS SECRETARY (SATURDAY): Jim Fox, 25 Coal Lane, Wolviston, Billingham, Stockton on Tees, TS22 5LW. Tel: 01740 644802 (H), 07779 985551 (M), 01740 654066 (B). Email: foxhealthsafety@hotmail.com
APPOINTMENTS SECRETARY (SUNDAY & MIDWEEK): David Swainson, 12 Upsall Grove, Fairfield, Stockton on Tees, TS19 7BH. Tel: 01642 645891 (H). Email: theswainsons@hotmail.com
ASSESSMENT & GRADING: Joe Doyle, 111 Throston Grange Lane, Hartlepool, TS26 0TZ. Tel: 01429 299243 (H), 07759 321769 (M). Email: joe.doyle@ntlworld.com
SADO: John F. Heselwood, 7 Mickleton Close, Great Lumley, Chester le Street, DH3 4SN. Tel: 0191 388 8671 (H). Email: johnheselwood@hotmail.com
REGIONAL REFEREE TRAINER (NORTH): Malcolm Shorney, 5 The Paddock, Middleton-St-George, Darlington, DL2 1BT. Tel: 01325 332773 (H). Email: malcolmshorney@rfu.com

Northumberland – 1893
PRESIDENT/CHAIRMAN/ASSESSMENT & GRADING/SADO: Bob Ward, 79 Grange Road, Morpeth, Northumberland, NE61 2UE. Tel: 01670 503991 (H), 07788 566479 (M), 01670 503015 (B). Fax: 01670

504188. Email: nor.ref@tlak21.com

SECRETARY/RECRUITMENT & RETENTION: Malcolm Jarvie, c/o Northumberland Resource Centre, Northern RFC. McCracken Park, Great North Road, Gosforth, Newcastle upon Tyne, NE3 2DG. Tel: 0191 251 3590 (H), 07816 416028 (M), 0191 281 8486 (B). Fax: 0191 236 3356. Email: nor.ref@talk21.com

FINANCE: Geoff Parkinson, 16 Sturdee Gardens, Jesmond, Newcastle upon Tyne, NE2 3QT. Tel: 0191 285 9431 (H). Email: geoff@parki1.fsnet.co.uk

T & D MANAGER: David Routledge, Cockle Park Farm, Morpeth, Northumberland, NE61 3EB. Tel: 01670 790929 (H), 07791 012105 (M), 01670 790227 (B). Fax: 01670 790929. Email: refroutledge@aol.com

APPOINTMENTS SECRETARY (WEEKENDS): Martin Page, 25 Hillcrest, Whitley Bay, Tyne and Wear, NE25 9AD. Tel: 0191 251 0748 (H). Fax: 0191 251 0748

APPOINTMENTS SECRETARY (MIDWEEK): Mike Hopper, 19 Briarsyde, Benton, Newcastle upon Tyne, NE12 9SL. Tel: 0191 270 2098 (H). Fax: 0191 292 1281. Email: mikehopper@bushinternet.com

DISCIPLINE: Kingsley Hyland OBE, 5 Hall Garth, Bridge Park, Gosforth, Newcastle, NE3 2DY. Tel: 0191 285 4997 (H), 07775 842596 (M), 0191 260 4233 (B). Email: khyland@talk21.com

EXCHANGE SECRETARY: Peter Howe, 6 Burnland Terrace, Hexham, Northumberland, NE46 3JT. Tel: 01434 606533 (H), 07802 433149 (M), 01670 534082 (B). Email: phowe@northumberland.gov.uk

ACTIVE REFEREES REP: Mark Sharpe, 24 Davenport Drive, Brunton Park, Newcastle upon Tyne, NE3 5AE. Tel: 0191 217 0681 (H), 01661 869902 (B). Email: sharpey@refman.freeserve.co.uk

CHAIRMAN OF SOCIAL: Alan Beddis, Two Cottages, Stelling Farm, Newton, Stocksfield, Northumberland. Tel: 01661 842267 (H), 0191 273 9635 (B)

SPONSORSHIP: Les Gutteridge, c/o Northumberland Resource Centre, Northern RFC, McCracken Park, Great North Road, Gosforth, Newcastle upon Tyne, NE3 2DG. Tel: 0191 266 0719 (H), 07866 630059 (M). Email: nor.ref@talk21.com

Cumbria – 1921

PRESIDENT: Tony Cunningham, 17 Carlton Road, Workington

CHAIRMAN/APPOINTMENTS: Mike Firby, 8 Fell View, Branthwaite, Workington, Cumbria, CA14 4SY. Tel: 01900 605631 (H), 01900 68141 (B), 07831 245888 (M). Fax: 01900 65075

SECRETARY: Alan Jenkinson, 39 James Street, Workington, Cumbria, CA14 2DF. Tel: 01900 68960 (H), 01900 733366 (B)

SADO: Bill Lee, 18 Rheda Park, Frizington, Cumbria, CA26 3TA. Tel: 01946 815617 (H)

EXCHANGES: Jim Thompson, 36 Queens Avenue, Seaton, Workington, CA14 1DL. Tel: 01900 62367 (H)

TREASURER: Rod Erlston, Eryi, Broughton Park, Cockermouth, CA13 0XW. Tel: 01900 824594 (H)

ASSISTANT SECRETARY: Ian Langley, Kiln Green House, Aikton, Wigton, Cumbria, CA7 0HY. Tel: 01697 344900 (H)

TRAINING OFFICERS: TBA

NORTH WEST FEDERATION OF RUGBY UNION REFEREES' SOCIETIES

CHAIRMAN/RFRU REPRESENTATIVE: Roger Bowden, 32 Carnoustie Close, Fulwood, Preston, Lancashire PR2 7ER. Tel: 01772 861167 (H) 07811 161706 (M). Fax: 01772 866032. Email: roger.bowden@lineone.net

SECRETARY: Allan Townsend, 57 Preston Road, Lytham St. Annes, Lancashire, FY8 5BN. Tel: 01253 735605 (H), 07960 139826 (M). Fax: 01253 735605. Email: allantownsend@lineone.net

FINANCE: Alan Worthington, 21 Sefton Gardens, Aughton, Ormskirk, Lancashire, L39 6RY. Tel: 01695 423762 (H). Email: 21aaw@onetel.com

CO-ORDINATOR: Geraint Davies, 3 Sambourne Fold, Ainsdale, Southport PR8 2SQ. Tel: 01704 575270 (H). Fax: 01704 575270. Email: gandmdavies@tesco.net/geraintdavies@rfu.com

Member Societies

Furness & District – 1948

PRESIDENT: Richard Knowles, The Old Barn, 111 Burneside Road, Kendal, Cumbria, LA9 6DZ.
Tel: 01539 723741 (H)
CHAIRMAN: Andy Hampshire, Southfield, 55 Milnthorpe Road, Kendal, Cumbria, LA9 5QG.
Tel: 01539 734372 (H)
SECRETARY/PR/DISCIPLINE: Nigel Rimmer, 2A Birkett Hill Cottages, Bowness-on-Windermere,
Cumbria, LA23 3ET. Tel: 01539 448230 (H), 01539 790054 (B). Email: n.rimmer@gilkes.com
TREASURER: Tony McAteer, 24 Hill Road, Barrow-in-Furness, Cumbria, LA14 4HA. Tel: 01229 432601 (H)
RECRUITMENT/B GRADE, C GRADE, NAT FOUND, 15-A-SIDE TRAINER: Steve Holmes, 2 Stoney
Lane, Galgate, Nr Lancaster, LA2 0JY. Tel: 01524 752876 (H), 07818 016140 (M). Email:
furnessref@aol.com
APPOINTMENTS SECRETARY: Dan Shovelton, 10 Buttermere Drive, Millom, Cumbria, LA18 4PL.
Tel: 01229 773743 (H), 07810 267153 (M)
MATCH SECRETARY/APPOINTMENTS/EXCHANGE SECRETARY: Peter Harney, 71 Furness Park
Road, Barrow-in-Furness, Cumbria, LA14 5PY. Tel: 01229 832898 (H)
ASSESSMENT AND GRADING: Mike Neal, 75 Fairgarth Drive, Kirkby Lonsdale, Cumbria, LA6 2FB.
Tel: 01524 271085 (H), 01539 446891 (B)
NORTH WEST FED REPS: John Gibson, 25 St James Drive, Burton-In-Kendal, Cumbria, LA6 1HY.
Tel: 01524 782186 (H), 07974 126859 (M)
John Mohammed, 2 Plumtree Bank, Heversham, Cumbria, LA7 7EF. Tel: 01539 563315 (H)

Liverpool & District – 1907

PRESIDENT: Alan Worthington, 21 Sefton Gardens, Aughton, Ormskirk, L39 6RY. Tel: 01695 423762.
Email: 21aaw@onetel.com
CHAIRMAN: Tony Rossall, 169 Pensby Road, Heswall, Wirral CH61 6UB. Tel: 0151 342 4221 (H), 0151
355 8445 (B). Fax: 0151 342 4221. Email: tony.rossall@btinternet.com
SECRETARY: Martin Buck, 32 Millfield Lane, Tarporley, Cheshire, CW6 0BF. Tel: 01829 730434 (H),
07867 616185 (M). Email: buckie.ref1@virgin.net
CHAIRMAN OF FINANCE: Dave Edmunds, 24 Alistair Drive, Bromborough, Wirral, CH63 0LH.
Tel: 0151 334 3792 (H), 0151 651 3002 (B). Fax: 0151 651 3091. Email: daveedmunds@ntlworld.com
RECRUITMENT & RETENTION: Clive Parker, 61 Bold Lane, Aughton, Ormskirk, L39 6SG. Tel: 01695
422269 (H). Email: blogwins@yahoo.com
PR: David Matthews, 15 Highfield Drive, Crank, St. Helens, Merseyside, WA11 7SE. Tel: 01744 889117
(H), 01744 20511 (B), 07787 548635 (M). Fax: 01744 20543. Email: david-helen@talk21.com
T&D MANAGER/NATIONAL FOUNDATION: Eddie Davies, 58 Coronation Drive, Crosby, Liverpool,
L23 3BP. Tel: 0151 924 0211 (H). Email: edaref@aol.com
DEVELOPMENT REFEREE TRAINER/B GRADE: Geraint Davies, 3 SAmbourn Fold, Ainsdale,
Southport, PR8 2SQ. Tel: 01704 575270 (H). Email: dandmdavies@tesco.net
C GRADE TRAINER: Mike Taylor, 139 Elliott Street, Tyldesley, Manchester, M9 8FL. Tel: 01942 797631 (H)
APPTS SECRETARY (WEEKENDS): Len Galey, 34 Mill Hill Road, Irby, Wirral CH61 4UF. Tel: 0151
648 3566 (H), 07808 776796 (M). Email: galey@tesco.net
APPTS SECRETARY (MIDWEEK): Jim Heaney, 20 Grangeside, Liverpool, L25 3PP. Tel: 0151 724 2087
(H). Email: jameseheaney@hotmail.com
RE-APPTS SECRETARY: Bob Smith, 76 Cunningham Drive, Bromborough, Wirral CH63 0JZ. Tel: 0151
200 8299 (H). Email: bobbet@lineone.net
DISCIPLINE: Mike Toole, 53 Leach Lane, Sutton Leach, St. Helens WA9 4PX. Tel: 01744 816497 (H),
07803 230211 (M). Email: mdtoole10@hotmail.com
ASSESSMENT & GRADING: Colin Christy, Upper Glenthorne, The Serpentine South, Blundellsands,
Liverpool, L23 6TB. Tel: 0151 924 3363 (H). Email: Joanna@stevebareham.demon.co.uk
SADO: David Yorke, 1a, Sandown Terrace, Boughton, Chester, CH3 5BN. Tel: 01244 344026 (H). Email:
dandmyorke@aol.com

Manchester & District – 1902

PRESIDENT: Peter Hughes, Higham, Burnley, Lancashire, BB12 9BU. Tel: 01282 771120 (H&B), 07771 711405 (M). Fax: 01282 779529. Email: ofpeh.higham@virgin.net

CHAIRMAN/PR: Roger Bowden, 32 Carnoustie Close, Preston, Lancashire, PR2 7ER. Tel: 01772 861167 (H), 07811 161706 (M). Fax: 01772 866032. Email: roger.bowden@lineone.net

SECRETARY/MINI/MIDI TRAINER/DISCIPLINE: Geoffrey A Gill, 45 Eskdale Avenue, Bramhall, Cheshire, SK7 1DX. Tel: 0161 439 5624 (H), 07891 002393 (M). Fax: 0161 439 5624. Email: geoffgill@virgin.net

FINANCE: Steve Halliday, Laneside, Wallbank Road, Bramhall, Stockport, Cheshire, SK7 3AP. Tel: 0161 439 6451 (H), 07989 951658 (M). Email: stevehalliday@aafoods.eu.com RECRUITMENT: John Jeskins, 5 Hazel Drive, Moss Nook, Manchester, M22 5LY. Tel: 0161 436 4807 (H), 0161 486 4676 (B). Fax: 0161 482 8129. Email: john.jeskins@btopenworld.com

RETENTION OFFICER: Brian S Smith, 2A Oak Avenue, Royton, Oldham, Lancashire, OL2 6TB. Tel: 0161 628 5393 (H), 07792 662639 (M). Email: brian@sprayshop.demon.co.uk

TRAINING & DEVELOPMENT MANAGER/NATIONAL FOUNDATION TRAINER: Geoff Cove, 18 Princes Road, Sale, Cheshire, M33 3FF. Tel: 0161 962 9371 (H), 07949 140305 (M), 0161 295 2334 (B). Fax: 0161 295 2332 (B). Email: g@cove.u-net.com

B GRADE/C GRADE/NATIONAL FOUNDATION TRAINER: David W Guerin, The Laurels, Brick Bank Lane, Allostock, Knutsford, Cheshire, WA16 9LZ. Tel: 01477 534194 (H), 07743 785774 (M). Email: david.guerin@talk21.com

APPT. SECRETARY (WEEKENDS)/RE-APPOINTMENTS SECRETARY: Paul Johnston, 2 Opal Close, Thornton Cleveleys, Lancashire, FY5 3LL. Tel: 01253 855486 (H), 07986 740764 (M), 01772 858634 (B). Fax: 01253 862642. Email: paul.johnston2004@btinternet.com

APPOINTMENTS SECRETARY (MIDWEEK/WEEKENDS)/EXCHANGE SECRETARY: Colin Durkin, 20 Great Acre, Whelley, Wigan, Lancashire, WN1 3NR. Tel: 01942 230693 (H), 07762 112801 (M)

RE-APPOINTMENTS SECRETARIES: Andy Dawson, 21 Rowan Croft, Clayton-le-Woods, Chorley, Lancashire, PR6 7UU. Tel: 01772 322778 (H), 07710 873093 (M), 01772 225591 (B). Email: andyand-suedaw@btinternet.com

Rob Sheard, 8 Douglas Drive, Heysham, Lancashire, LA3 2LN. Tel: 01524 855270 (H), 07766 338980 (M), 01524 850506 (B). Email: robsheard@madref.fsnet.co.uk

John Harries, Gwynant, 39 Wallingford Road, Wilmslow. Cheshire, SK9 3JT. Tel: 01625 524359 (H), 07946 894253 (M), 01204 703782 (B). Fax: 01625 524359. Email: jananjon@ic24.net

Myles Kitchiner, 67 Crofton Avenue, Timperley, Altrincham, Cheshire, WA15 6BZ. Tel: 0161 973 3003 (H), 07966 447546 (M), 0161 4936 4148 (B). Fax: 0161 973 3003. Email: myles@kitchiner.freeserve.co.uk

ASSESSMENT & GRADING: Paul Watkins, 3 Pexhill Drive, Macclesfield, Cheshire, SK10 3LP. Tel: 01625 610597 (H), 01625 515211 (B). Email: paul.watkins@astrazeneca.com (B), paw001@ntlworld.com (H)

SADO: Geoffrey Elliott, 4 Overdale Road, Romiley, Stockport, Cheshire, SK6 3HL. Tel: 0161 430 6000 (H&B), 07850 406 036 (M). Fax: 0161 355 5206. Email: geoffelliott@ntlworld.com

YORKSHIRE FEDERATED SOCIETY OF REFEREES

CHAIRMAN: Murray Halliday, 30 Hunters Way, Dringhouses, York, YO24 1JJ. Tel: 01904 700837 (H), 07808 801025 (M). Email: murray.halliday@btinternet.com

SECRETARY/PR/DISCIPLINE: Mike Wells, 36 Kings Meadow Mews, Wetherby, LS22 7FT. Tel: 01937 582114 (H), 07778 413103 (M). Email: mikewells5864848@aol.com

FINANCE: Stewart Mitchell, 5 St. Anthony's Park, Hedon, Hull, HU12 8NU. Tel: 01482 896299 (H). Email: stewartmitchell@hedon77.freeserve.co.uk

RECRUITMENT & RETENTION: Matthew Haley, 18 Woods Court, Harrogate. Tel: 07946 405604 (M). Email: matthew.haley@btopenworld.com

T&D MANAGER/B GRADE/C GRADE/NATIONAL FOUNDATION/15-A-SIDE/MINI-MIDI TRAINER: Steve Hayne, 18 Millbank View, Pudsey, Leeds, LS28 9NN. Tel: 0113 204 0002 (H). Email: Stevehayne48231@aol.com

FEDERATION APPOINTMENTS OFFICER: Jim Turner, 67 Greenville Drive, Bradford, BD12 0PT.
Tel: 01274 679976 (H). Email: j.m.c.turner@bradford.ac.uk
RFRU REPRESENTATIVE/FEDERATION COACHING CO-ORDINATOR: Allan MacGregor, 71
Ellers Avenue, Bessacarr, Doncaster, DN4 7DZ. Tel: 01302 538584 (H), 07703 181872 (M). Email:
mcgregor@globalnet.co.uk
EXCHANGE SECRETARY: Sam Young, 17 Town Moor Avenue, Doncaster, DN2 6BN. Tel: 01302
323367 (H), 07778 402777 (M). Email: shy@argonet.co.uk
ASSESSMENT & GRADING: Peter Farrell, 276 Horbury Road, Wakefield, WF2 8QU. Tel: 01924
369680 (H). Email: peter.farrell@btinternet.com
DEVELOPMENT SQUAD CO-ORDINATOR: Tom White, 'Southwood', 12 Sowood Lane, Ossett, WF5
0LE. Tel: 01924 273786 (H). Email: tom136white@aol.com

Member Societies

Central Yorkshire – 1981
CHAIRMAN: Rob Staines, 23 Bramham Park Court, Middleton, Leeds, LS10 4UL. Tel: 0113 2770713
(H), 07860 951852 (M). Email: robs@bayford.co.uk
SECRETARY/DISCIPLINE: Mark Walker, 12 Bracken Edge, Leeds, LS8 4EE. Tel: 0113 262 5315 (H),
07762 054223 (M). Email: spitfire_1962@tesco.net
FINANCE: David Downham, 11 Stainburn Mount, Leeds, LS17 6NW. Tel: 0113 272 1548 (H), 07739
517169 (M). Email: david@pharmacy2u.co.uk
RECRUITMENT & RETENTION OFFICER: Matthew Haley, 18 Woods Court, Harrogate, North
Yorkshire. Tel: 07939 722910 (M). Email: matthew.haley@btopenworld.com
T&D MANAGER: Nick Mashender, 75 Wood Park View, Barnsley, S71 3NL. Tel: 01226 290623 (H),
07811 323487 (B). Email: nick.mashender@beaumont-legal.co.uk
APPOINTMENTS OFFICER: Nick Mashender, 75 Wood Park View, Barnsley, S71 3NL. Tel: 01226
290623 (H), 07811 323487 (B). Email: nick.mashender@beaumont-legal.co.uk
APPTS SECRETARY (MIDWEEK): Tony Hockney, 31 Hammerton Drive, Garforth, Leeds, LS25 2BJ.
Tel: 0113 286 9130 (H), 07775 865117 (M). Email: tony.hockney@virgin.net
RE-APPTS SECRETARY: Phil Shaw, 3 Holly Park, Horsforth, Leeds, LS18 5US. Tel: 0113 239 0179 (H),
07720 814415 (M). Email: shawwpp@btinternet.com
ASSESSMENT & GRADING/SADO: Chris Younger, 293 Denby Dale Road, Wakefield WF2 7BQ.
Tel: 01924 363840 (H). Email: youngec01@leedslearning.net
APPOINTMENTS SECRETARY (SUNDAY): Dick Cowley, 15 St Andrews Close, Leeds, LS13 1JE.
Tel: 01132 564644 (H), 07748 546988 (M). Email: rcowley@btopenworld.com

East Yorkshire
CHAIRMAN/COACHING CO-ORDINATOR: Terry Hardaker, 130 Yapham Road, Pocklington, YO4
2DY. Tel: 01759 303619 (H), 07940 036640 (M). Email: twhardaker@aol.com
SECRETARY/PR: Peter Hardman, 'The Old Forge', 57 Norwood Grove, Beverley, HU17 9HR. Tel: 01482
871076 (H), 07989 978815 (M). E-mail: petehard@hotmail.com/phardman@connexionshumber.co.uk
FINANCE: Stewart Mitchell, 5 St Anthony's Park, Hedon, HU12 8NU. Tel: 01482 896229 (H), 07808
103372 (M). Email: stewartmitchell@hedon77.freeserve.co.uk
RECRUITMENT: Brian Davison, 7 Hobson Road, Elloughton, Brough, HU15 1JS. Tel: 01482 665310
(H), 01724 296742 (B), 07976 072356 (M). Email: beekaydee7@yahoo.co.uk
T&D MANAGER: Andrew Crozier, 5 Matson Road, Bridlington, YO16 4SZ. Tel: 07739 179142 (M)
APPOINTMENTS: Matthew Daubney, 11 St. Abbs Close, Victoria Dock, Hull, HU9 1TX. Tel: 01482
225770 (H), 01430 478445 (B), 07795 234 692 (M). Email: referee@vikdock.karoo.co.uk
EXCHANGE/RE-APPTS & SUNDAY SECRETARY: John Clayton, 45 Chestnut Avenue, Willerby, Hull
HU10 6PD. Tel: 01482 651667 (H), 07775 755758 (M), 08707 513403 (B). Fax: 08707 513131. Email:
jclayton@lewisgroup.co.uk
MID-WEEK APPOINTMENTS: Phil Padgett, 'Bladonia', Bladons Walk, Kirkella, Hull, HU10 7AX.
Tel: 01482 651335 (H), 07890 608821 (M). Email: Padgett@padgett.karoo.co.uk
ASSESSMENT & GRADING: Ken Metcalf, 21 Gillshill Road, Hull, HU8 0JG. Tel: 01482 704341 (H),

07710 684090 (M)

North Yorks & Cleveland

CHAIRMAN/RECRUITMENT & RETENTION/EXCHANGES/ RE-APPTS SECRETARY: John Fisher, Cherry Tree Cottage, High Street, Whixley, York, YO26 8AW. Tel: 01423 331031 (H), 07712 384786 (M). Fax: 01423 331031. Email: fishers@clara.co.uk
SECRETARY/DISCIPLINE: Bob Scott, 26 Nunthorpe Avenue, York, YO23 1PF. Tel: 01904 653475 (H), 07711 326829 (M). Email: Bob@scott5488.fsnet.co.uk
FINANCE: Russ Warin, 53 Rawcliffe Lane, York, YO30 5SJ. Tel : 01904 653462 (H), 07887 672018 (M). Email : russ.warin@spcorp.com
T&D MANAGER/B GRADE, C GRADE, NAT FOUND, 15-A-SIDE, MINI/MIDI TRAINER: Jonathan Hill, Piggywidden, Seven Wells, Amotherby, Malton, YO17 6TT. Tel: 01653 699877 (H), 07971 119107 (M). Email: jont.hill@talk21.com
APPTS SECRETARY (WEEKENDS & MIDWEEK): David Slawson, 4 Bracken Road, Dringhouses, York, YO24 1JT. Tel: 01904 705460 (H), 01904 455169 (B). Email: david@bellywave.freeserve.co.uk
GRADING SECRETARY/COACHING CO-ORDINATOR: Sydney Goodall, 41 Gordon Crescent, Richmond, North Yorkshire, DL10 5AQ. Tel: 01748 824016 (H), 07876 768826 (M), 01904 442933 (B). Email: sidgoodall@aol.com
WHISTLERS TROPHY SECRETARY: Mike Harrison, The Sycamore, 12 Millfield Lane, Nether Poppleton, York, YO26 6HR. Tel: 01904 793457 (H), 01609 785711 (B). Fax: 01609 776149. Email: mike.harrison@northyorks.gov.uk

South Yorkshire

CHAIRMAN: Cliff Sidebottom, 13 Florence Rise, Darfield, Barnsley S73 9PW. Tel: 01226 754066 (H). Email: c_sidebottom2000@yahoo.com
SECRETARY & FINANCE/PR/DISCIPLINE/PR: Allan MacGregor, 71 Ellers Avenue, Doncaster DN4 7DZ. Tel: 01302 538584 (H), 07703 181872 (M), 01302 533588 (B). Fax: 01302 533588. Email: mcgregor@globalnet.co.uk
RECRUITMENT & RETENTION OFFICER: Adrian John, 50 Common Lane, Tickhill, Doncaster, DN11 9UN. Tel: 01302 759987 (H), 07778 148202 (M). Email: akbjohn@gotadsl.co.uk
T&D MANAGER: Kevan Crawshaw, 63 Worksop Road, South Anston, Sheffield, S31 7ET. Tel: 01909 567290 (H). Email: kevan.crawshaw@hmps.gsi.gov.uk
APPTS SECRETARY (SATURDAYS): Andy Baker, 16 Lidget Close, Aston Manor, Sheffield, S26 4ST. Tel: 01142 549001 (H), 07733 300564 (M). Email: abterminal@btinternet.com
APPTS SECRETARY (MIDWEEK): As Chairman
APPTS SECRETARY (SUNDAYS): Nick Williams, Aston Hall, Hope Valley, Derbyshire, S33 6RA. Tel: 01433 621288 (H), 01142 738216 (B). Email: ndowill@aol.com
GRADINGS SECRETARY: Ron Perry, 39 Marchwood Road, Sheffield S6 5LB. Tel: 0114 234 4066 (H). Email: rhp@a-and-d-firstaid.co.uk
SADO & ASSESSMENTS: Pat Williamson, 83 Dovedale Road, Rotherham S65 3AW. Tel: 01709 518574 (H), 07730 204099 (M). Email: pgw.83ddr@virgin.net
EXCHANGES SECRETARY: Sam Young, 17 Town Moor Avenue, Doncaster, DN2 6BN. Tel: 01302 323367 (H), 07778 402777 (M). Email: shy@argonet.co.uk

West Yorkshire

CHAIRMAN: John Lister, Trinity House, Harrison Road, Halifax, HX1 2QR. Tel: 01422 369255 (H), 01422 363498 (B), 07770 568164 (M). Fax: 01422 321071. Email: mail@php-group.co.uk
SECRETARY: John Phillips, 'West Croft', Hebden Road, Haworth, BD22 8RS. Tel: 01535 645742 (H), 07721 562437 (M). Email: jfphllps@aol.com
FINANCE/RECRUITMENT & RETENTION: Jerome Murphy, 18 Plane Tree Nest, Halifax, HX2 7PR. Tel: 01422 346292 (H), 07931 967936 (M). Email: jeromemurphy@tinyonline.co.uk
T&D MANAGER: Jason Brian, 90 Sapgate Lane, Thornton, Bradford, BD13 3DY. Tel: 01274 832697 (H), 01274 472162 (B), 07989 181880 (M). Email: jrbrian@ybs.co.uk
APPOINTMENTS SECRETARY: Jim Turner, 67 Greenville Drive, Bradford, BD12 0PT. Tel: 01274

679976 (H). Fax: 01274 235350. Email: j.m.c.turner@bradford.ac.uk

RE-APPOINTMENTS/EXCHANGE SEC: Ian Boyd, 23 Walkers Green, Wortley, Leeds, LS12 4UN. Tel: 0113 279 7094 (H), 07803 937395 (M). Email: ianboydrtd@hotmail.com

APPOINTMENTS SECRETARY (MIDWEEK)/COACH CO-ORDINATOR: Mike Tasker, 2 Lodge Hill Road, Ossett, WF5 9RU. Tel: 01924 218854 (H), 07812 660837 (M). Email: mt014j2602@blueyonder.co.uk

GRADING: Alan Twigger, 'Brankstone', Chantry Drive, Ilkley, LS29 9HV. Tel: 01943 602612 (H)

EASTERN COUNTIES RUGBY UNION REFEREES FEDERATION

PRESIDENT: John Adler, Vellator, 4 Green Close, Springfield, Chelmsford, Essex, CM1 7SL. Tel: 01245 259531 (H). Email: vellator@aol.com

CHAIRMAN: Chris Shutie, 140 Kingswood Avenue, Thorpe Marriott, Norwich, Norfolk, NR8 6UR. Tel: 01603 260403 (H), 07970 341166 (M), 01603 260403 (B). Email: chris@chris-shutie.co.uk

SECRETARY: Alan Gold, 6 Boxted Close, Buckhurst Hill, Essex, IG9 6BX. Tel: 0208 281 1041 (H), 07744 435412 (M). Email: agold@lineone.net

TREASURER: Ian Stewart, 7 Minster Road, Haverhill, Suffolk, CB9 0DR. Tel: 01440 706076 (H). Email: iandmstewart@btinternet.com

TRAINING & DEVELOPMENT: David Locke, 8 Swan Meadow, Lower Street, Stratford St. Mary, Suffolk, CO7 6JQ. Tel: 01206 323944 (H), 07765 228360 (M). Email: davidlocke@rfu.com

APPOINTMENTS/RE-APPOINTMENTS SEC: Paddy Lockwood, 2 Third Avenue, Glemsford, Sudbury, Suffolk, CO10 7QJ. Tel: 01787 280700 (H), 07884 313898 (M). Email: paddy.lockwood@virgin.net

CHAIRMAN OF APPOINTMENTS/EXCHANGE SECRETARY: Mike Stott, Brick Kiln Farm, North Walsham, Norfolk, NR28 9LH. Tel: 01692 409043 (H), 07787 903366 (M). Email: mikestott@tesco.net

ASSESSMENT & GRADING: Viv Hathaway, 253 Oulton Road, Oulton Village, Lowestoft, Suffolk, NR32 4QX. Tel: 01502 574259 (H), Email: cuddlytaff@supanet.com

SOUTH EAST GROUP REF: Paul Storey, 26 The Green, Mendlesham, Stowmarket, Suffolk, IP14 5RQ. Tel: 01449 767136 (H). Email: paul.storey@lsc.gov.uk

Member Societies

Essex – 1961

PRESIDENT/APPTS (MIDWEEK): Ken Morgan, 3 Crammerville Walk, Rainham, Essex, RM13 9PS. Tel: 01708 520317 (H), 0207 582 6975 (B), 07771 448508 (M)

CHAIRMAN: Alistair Newton, 98 Clockhouse Lane, Collier Row, Romford, Essex, RM5 3QT. Tel: 01708 704563 (H), 0208 217 5355 (B). Email: alinewton98@netscape.net

SECRETARY/RECRUITMENT: Alan Gold, 6 Boxstead Close, Buckhurst Hill, Essex, IG9 6BX. Tel: 0208 281 1041 (H), 07744 435412 (M). Email: agold@lineone.net

TREASURER: Paul Jackson, 'Stanhill', North Hill, Little Baddow, Essex, CM3 4TD. Tel: 01245 223562 (H). Email: littlebaddow@virgin.net

APPOINTMENTS SECRETARY: David Walker, 35 Church Road, Wickham Bishops, Witham, Essex, CM8 3JZ. Tel: 01621 892607 (H), 07986 638029 (M). Email: davewalker@ggsworld.com.

TRAINING OFFICER/ECRURF REPRESENTATIVE: Dean Ford, 14 Boleyn Way, Boreham, Chelmsford, Essex, CM3 3JJ. Tel: 01245 461113 (H), 07751 507539 (M). Email: forddmb@aol.com

RE-APPTS (SATURDAY)/ESSEX COMMITTEE REP/GRADINGS (ALL REPORTS): Eric McLaughlan, 17 Halsham Crescent, Barking, Essex, IG11 9HG. Tel: 0208 594 4576 (H). Email: eric@mclaughlan.fsbusiness.co.uk

Norfolk – 1953

PRESIDENT: Alan Gibbs, 6 Hillview Road, Sheringham, Norfolk. Tel: 01263 820088 (H). Email:

alangill.gibbs@virgin.net
SECRETARY/RECRUITMENT: Graham Cross, Manor Farm, Roydon, Diss, IP22 5QS. Tel: 01379 642345 (H), 07850 642345 (M). Fax: 01379 650850. Email: graham.ccross@virgin.net
FINANCE: Ken Hutchins, Diamond H Controls Ltd, Vulcan Rd North, Norwich, NR6 6AH. Tel: 01603 254906 (B). Fax: 01603 788440. Email: kenh@diamond-h.com
T&D MANAGER: Viv Hathaway, 253 Oulton Road, Lowestoft, Suffolk, NR32 4QX. Tel: 01502 574259 (H). Email: cuddlytaff@supanet.com
B GRADE TRAINER: As Secretary/Recruitment
APPTS SECRETARY (WEEKENDS): Terry Ellans, 47 St. Nicholas Street, Thetford, IP24 1BG. Tel: 01842 753506 (H), 07811 580306 (M). Email: terence.ellans@tesco.net
DISCIPLINE: via Eastern Counties
ASSESSMENT & GRADING: Mark Salter, Sgts' Mess, Wattingsham Airfield, Ipswich, Suffolk, IP7 7RA. Tel: 01449 744599 (H), 01449 728986 (B), 07733 217284 (M). Email: markwsalter@hotmail.com
REFEREE HOTLINE: 07876 657007. Website: www.ecrefs.org

Suffolk & North Essex

PRESIDENT: Roy Marfleet, Lilac House, Waldingfield Road, Chilton, Sudbury, Suffolk, CO10 0PP. Tel: 01787 375350 (H), 07780 997832 (M). Email: roy@mdscivileng.co.uk
SECRETARY: Darryl Chapman, 5 Bridge Street, Stowmarket, Suffolk, IP14 1PP. Tel: 01449 672787 (H), 07775 817437 (M). Email: darryl.chapman@dowcorning.com
TREASURER: Ian Stewart, 7 Minster Road, Haverhill, Suffolk, CB9 0DR: Tel: 01440 706076 (H), 0771 469 6708 (M). Email: ian@stewie.go-plus.net
TRAINING/RECRUITMENT & RETENTION: Nick White, 5 Gainsborough Road, Sudbury, Suffolk, CO10 2HT. Tel: 01787 378477 (H). Email: nickwhite@hotmail.com
APPOINTMENTS/SADO: Paddy Lockwood, 2 Third Avenue, Glemsford, Sudbury, Suffolk, CO10 7QJ. Tel: 01787 280700 (H). Email: paddy.lockwood@virgin.net
RE-APPOINTMENTS: Steve Tatum, 15 Western Avenue, Silver End, Witham, Essex, CM8 3SA. Tel: 07932 150390 (M). Email: steve_tatum@yahoo.co.uk

SOUTH EAST FEDERATION

CHAIRMAN: John Masters, The Owls, 18 Butlers Road, Horsham, West Sussex, RH13 6AJ. Tel: 01403 264973 (H), 01403 755000 (B), 07778 642122 (M). Email: jrm.ssrfur@tiscali.co.uk
SECRETARY: Iain Mitchell, 26 Little Bridges Close, Southwater, Horsham, West Sussex, RH13 9HH. Tel: 01403 731716 (H), 07909 962085 (M), 01293 423690 (B). Fax: 01293 423698. Email: iainmitchell@tinyonline.co.uk
FINANCE: Nick Robinson, 3 Balmoral Gardens, Sanderstead, Surrey, CR2 0HN. Tel: 0208 4091980 (H), 07957 362910 (M), 020 8651 7022 (B). Fax: 020 8651 7029. Email: nickrob@clara.net
T&D MANAGER/B GRADE TRAINER: Dave Broadwell c/o RFU
APPOINTMENTS SECRETARY (WEEEKENDS)/(MIDWEEK)/ RE-APPTS: Phil Bowers, 17 Bluebell Close, East Grinstead, RH19 1RS. Tel: 01342 317869 (H), 0207 404 4444 (B). Email: philbowersref@aol.com
RFUR REPRESENTATIVE/ASSESSOR CO-ORDNIATOR: Tim Fagg, Little Ranters Oast, Ranters Oak, Benenden Road, Rolvenden, Kent, TN17 4JE. Tel: 01580 243166 (H), 01233 648402 (B), 07799 118930 (M)

Kent – 1950

PRESIDENT/ ASSESSMENT & GRADING: Colin Blackham, 5 Turnstone, New Barn, Longfield, Kent, DA3 7NR. Tel: 01474 704576 (H). Email: grading@kentrefs.co.uk
CHAIRMAN: Alistair Cumming, 64 Prince Georges Avenue, Wimbledon, London, SW20 8BH. Tel: 020 8540 7365 (H), 07771 827166 (M). Email: chairman@kentrefs.co.uk
SECRETARY/APPTS SECRETARY/RECRUITMENT: Graeme Charters, 42 Ridgeway Crescent, Tonbridge, Kent, TN10 4NR. Tel: 01732 354851 (H), 07767 236666 (M), 01732 373900 (B). Fax: 08707 053313. Email: secretary@kentrefs.co.uk

FINANCE: Nick Robinson, 3 Balmoral Gardens, Sanderstead, South Croydon, Surrey, CR2 0HN. Tel: 0208 409 1980 (H), 07802 294477 (M), 0207 6395726 (B). Fax: 0208 4091979. Email: treasurer@kentrefs.co.uk

COURSE ADMINISTRATOR: Matthew Sellen, 20 Goldsmid Road, Tonbridge, Kent, TN9 2BX. Tel: 01732 350877 (H), 07876 035012 (M). E-mail: matthew.sellen@lexisnexis.co.uk

PR & COMMUNICATIONS: Nigel Meddemmen, 11 Wickenden Road, Orpington, Kent, BR6 0QP. Tel: 01732 460002 (H), 07860 482435 (M), 0208 646 7115 (B). Email: n.meddemmen@shuttlesound.com

DEVELOPMENT MANAGER: Terry Hall, 49 Goodwood Crescent, Singlewell, Gravesend, DA12 5EY. Tel: 01474 566238 (H), 07773 793996 (M). Email: othall@clara.net

RE-APPTS SECRETARY: Graham Fryer, The Marshalls, Leeds Road, Maidstone, Kent, ME17 3JG. Tel: 0700 2776468 (H&B)

DISCIPLINE: Bill Hobba, 53 Lansdowne Road, Tonbridge, Kent, TN9 1JD. Tel: 01732 771397 (H), 07715 485730 (M), 01474 833551 (B). Fax: 01474 832327. Email: discipline@kentrefs.co.uk

SADO: Andy Jordan, 54 Newstead Road, London, SE12 0TB. Tel: 0208 857 6284 (H), 07919 554058 (M), 0208 943 2157 (B). Email : advisor@kentrefs.co.uk

KIT: Owen Quantick, 81 Anne Boleyn Close, Eastcheap, Isle of Sheppey, Kent, ME12 4DJ. Tel: 01795 880334 (H), 07734 298682 (M), 01227 272362 (B). Email: kit@kentrefs.co.uk

Sussex – 1932

PRESIDENT/FINANCE: David Tree, East Wickham, 59 College Lane, Hurstpierpoint, BN6 9AD. Tel: 01273 832553 (H). Email: david@dgtree.fsnet.co.uk

CHAIRMAN/TRAINING & DEVELOPMENT/ALL COURSE: Philip Bowers, 17 Bluebell Close, East Grinstead, RH19 1RS. Tel: 01342 317869 (H), 0207 404 4444 (B). Email: philbowersref@aol.com

SECRETARY: Iain Mitchell, 26 Little Bridges Close, Southwater, Horsham, West Sussex, RH13 9HH. Tel: 01403 731716 (H), 07909 962085 (M), 01293 423690 (B). Fax: 01293 423698. Email: iainmitchell@tinyonline.co.uk

RECRUITMENT & RETENTION/PR: Michael Madden, 4 Park Rd, Burgess Hill, RH15 8ET. Tel: 01444 245295 (H), 01444 477497 (B), 07801 015922 (M). Email: michael.madden@ukgateway.net

APPTS MIDWEEK, WEEKENDS & RE-APPTS: David Maconachie, 20 Caledon Avenue, Felpham, Bognor Regis, PO22 7QZ. Tel: 01243 582924 (H). Email: dave-anne-mac@hotmail.com

DISCIPLINE (Sussex RFU): Roger Edmondson, 1 Ryefield Close, Little Ratton, Eastbourne, BN21 2XJ. Tel: 01323 501893 (H)

SADO: Rob Lowe, 9 Birch Tree Close, Emsworth, Hampshire, PO10 7SJ. Tel: 01243 375073 (H), 07967 338523 (M). Email: robtinalowe@hotmail.com

ASSESSMENT & GRADING: Mike Richardson, 6 Wayside, Westdene, Brighton, BN1 5HL. Tel: 01273 500512 (H), 07860 638092 (M), 0207 3771777 (B). Email: mr@railex.demon.co.uk

LONDON FEDERATION

London Society– 1889

GENERAL SECRETARY: Edward Evans, 7 Briar Walk, Putney, London, SW15 6UD. Tel: 0208 789 1347 (H), 0207 832 7047 (B). Fax: 0207 832 7589. Email: edward.evans@londonrugby.com

RFRU REPRESENTATIVE: Tony Trigg, Bovington Ash, Chipperfield Road, Bovingdon, Hemel Hemstead, Herts, HP3 0JW. Tel: 01442 832735 (H). Email: tony@jaftrigg.freeserve.co.uk

TREASURER: David Morgan, 6A Albert Square, London, SW8 1BT. Tel: 0207 587 0559 (H), 0207 212 3998 (B). Email: david.a.morgan@uk.pwc.com

ASSISTANT TREASURER: David Tyler, 14 Chart Close, Bromley, Kent, BR2 0EB. Tel: 0208 464 2372 (H)

ASSISTANT SECRETARY (ADMIN): Bob Jenkins, 37 March Court, Warwick Drive, Putney, London, SW15 6LE. Tel: 0208 789 3396 (H)

ASS. SEC. (ADVISERS) ALL. EXCH. REP/SADO: Clive Goff, 67 Ravenswood Crescent, Harrow, Middlesex, HA2 9JL. Tel: 0208 422 4906 (H)

ASSISTANT SEC. (EXCHANGES): Clive Morley, 1 Meadow Drive, Amersham, Bucks, HP6 6LB. Tel: 01494 724942 (H)

RECRUITMENT SECRETARY/TRAINING CO-ORDINATOR: Bob Ockenden, 19 Highbury Close,

New Malden, Surrey, KT3 5BY. Tel: 0208 949 4420 (H), 07979 797694 (M). Email: bobockenden@rfu.com

CHAIRMAN – APPTS & GRADING: Tim Miller, St Margaret's Lodge, 48 Ledborough Lane, Beaconsfield, Bucks, HP9 2DD. Tel: 01494 671702 (H), 07799 582646 (M). Email: tim.miller@ uk.standardchartered.com

CHAIRMAN – TRAINING & DEVELOPMENT: Graham Beaumont, 28 Manor Crescent, Surbiton, Surrey, KT5 8LQ. Tel: 0208 399 8353 (H), 0207 493 4933 (B). Email: graham.beaumont@kingsturge.co.uk

WEST REGIONAL MANAGER: Mark Powell, 33 Regatta Point, Kewbridge Road, Brentford, Middlesex, TW8 0EB. Tel: 0208 568 4250 (H)

NORTH REGIONAL MANAGER: Chris Rogers, 7 Hawksmoor Green, Hutton, Brentwood, Essex, CM13 1LE. Tel: 01277 221652 (H). Email: Chris.rogers@londonrugby.com

SOUTH WEST REGIONAL MANAGER: Will Mason, 31 Knightswood Crescent, New Malden, Surrey, KT3 5JR. Tel: 0208 949 5154 (H)

SOUTH EAST REGIONAL MANAGER: Steve Hancock, 8 Babbacombe Road, Bromley, BR1 3LW. Tel: 0208 464 5196 (H), 07976 317555 (M). Email: steve.hancock@londonrugby.com

MIDWEEK APPTS: Brian Gabb, 3 Mead Close, Egham, Surrey, TW20 8JA. Tel: 01784 740628 (H). Email: brian.gabb@londonrugby.com

Staines

SECRETARY/PR/RECRUITMENT: Richard Evans, 33 Castle Road, Isleworth, Middlesex, TW7 6QR. Tel: 0208 568 1185 (H), 07961 485898 (M). Email: Richardagillevans@yahoo.co.uk

FINANCE: Lynda Filer, 91 Hall Road, Isleworth. Tel: 0208 560 8504 (H)

TRAINING/ASSESSMENT & GRADING/SADO: Stewart Young, 8 Knowle Park Avenue, Staines, Middlesex, TW18 1AN. Tel: 01784 457159 (H). Email: stuartg.young@btopenworld.com

APPOINTMENTS SECRETARY/ RE-APPTS SECRETARY: Niall Adams, 91 Hall Road, Isleworth, Middlesex TW7 7PB. Tel: 0208 5608504 (H), 07776 580884 (B), 07811 425862 (M). Email: niall_adams@lineone.net

DISCIPLINE: As Training

SOUTHERN FEDERATION

CHAIRMAN: Roger Hancock, Sugarswell Bungalow, Shenington, Banbury, Oxon, OX15 6HW. Tel: 01295 670368 (H), 07932 080374 (M), 01295 270200 (B). Fax: 01295 271784. Email: rogerh@ whitleystimpson.co.uk

SECRETARY: Peter Downes, Coxboro Dell, High Road, Cookham, Berks, SL6 9HR. Tel: 01628 524881 (H), 0870 234 6831 (B), 07867 822008 (M). Email: pmdownes@btinternet.com

FINANCE: John Hawes, 32 Thames Crescent, Maidenhead, Berks, SL6 8EY. Tel: 01628 633847 (H), 07932 650898 (M). Fax: 01628 524881. Email: john.hawes@homehardware.biz

MODS REP/RFRU REP: Peter Topham, Timbuck, Nett Road, Shrewton, Salisbury, Wilts, SP3 4HB. Tel: 01980 620539 (H), 07752 380446 (M). Fax: 01980 620539. Email: peter@topham971.freeserve.co.uk

APPTS & EXCHANGES: David Levy, 40 Thames Crescent, Maidenhead, Berkshire, SL6 8EY. Tel: 01628 637781 (H), 07775 937914 (M), 0208 826 4610 (B). Fax: 01628 637781. Email: davidlevyrefs@supanet.com

TRAINING OFFICER: John Ford, 13 Warwick Close, Cox Green, Maidenhead, SL6 3AL. Tel: 01628 548680 (H), 0208 756 2186 (B). Email: john_ford@safeway.co.uk/john.ford@bsrfur.com

FSADO/ADVISING & GRADING: Jim Firth, 36 Columbine Road, Basingstoke, Hampshire, RG22 5RW. Tel: 01256 327526 (H). Email: james.firth2@btopenworld.com

RFU REP: Andy Melrose, 12 Folly Lane, Blandford St. Mary, Dorset, DT11 9QF. Email: andymelrose@rfu.com

Member Societies

Berkshire – 1948

CHAIRMAN: Andrew Harris, Rose Hall, Washpool, Swindon, SN5 3PN. Tel: 01793 772302 (H), 07801 922291 (M), 0118 981 1466 (B). Fax: 0118 981 4470. Email: andrewharris@clara.co.uk
SECRETARY/RECRUITMENT/DISCIPLNE: John Hawes, 32 Thames Crescent, Maidenhead, Berks SL6 8EY. Tel: 01628 633847 (H), 07932 650898 (M). Fax: 01628 633847. Email: john.hawes@homehardware.biz
FINANCE: Roger Naish, 44 Wilmington Close, Woodley, Berkshire, RG5 4LR. Tel: 0118 376 9797 (H), 07803 002786 (M), 0207 357 7888 (B). Fax: 0207 357 8855. Email: roger.naish@ntlworld.com
T&D MANAGER: John Ford, 13 Warwick Close, Cox Green, Maidenhead, Berks, SL6 3AL. Tel: 01628 548680 (H), 0208 756 2186 (B). Email: John.ford@bsrfur.com
APPTS SECRETARY: Simon Bourne, 41 Copse Close, Cippenham, Berkshire, SL1 5DT. Tel: 01753 511663 (H), 07759 644497 (M). Email: simon.bourne@bsrufr.com
EXCHANGE APPOINTMENTS: David Levy, 40 Thames Crescent, Maidenhead, Berks, SL6 8EY. Tel: 01628 637781 (H), 07775 937914 (M), 0207 796 8229 (B). Fax: 01628 637781. Email: Davidlevyrefs@supanet.com
APPTS SECRETARY (MIDWEEK) & RE-APPTS SECRETARY: Brian Reed, 214 Winchester Road, Basingstoke, Hants, RG21 8YR. Tel: 01256 353425 (H). Fax: 01256 353425
ASSESSMENT & GRADING: David Robertson, 21 Bannard Road, Maidenhead, SL6 4NP. Tel: 01628 634244 (H)
SADO: John Evans, 35 Spinfield Park, Marlow, Bucks, SL7 2DD. Tel: 01628 483711 (H). Fax: 01628 483711. Email: evansjohn@talk21.com

Buckinghamshire – 1960

PRESIDENT/DISCIPLINE: Ro Bates, Hamara, Spurlands End Road, Great Kingshill, High Wycombe, Bucks, HP15 6HX. Tel: 01494 713595 (H)
CHAIRMAN/T&D MANAGER: Peter Downes, Coxboro Dell, High Road, Cookham, Berks, SL6 9HR. Tel: 01628 524881 (H), 07867 822008 (M), 08702 346831 (B). Email: pmdownes@btinternet.com
SECRETARY: Richard Bobbett, 2 Cedar Ridge, Hyde Heath, Amersham, Buckinghamshire, HP6 5SF. Tel: 01494 773225 (H), 07768 505427 (M). Email: richardbobbett@aol.com
RECRUITMENT & RETENTION: Dave Allen, 28 Hemingway Road, Haydon Hill, Aylesbury, Bucks, HP19 8SD. Tel: 01296 381881 (H), 07801 860243 (M). Email: david@allen432.freeserve.co.uk
FINANCE: Adrian Lewis, c/o Major Financial Groups Division, FSA, 25 North Colonnade, London, E14 5HS. Tel: 07711 423760 (M), 0207 676 1830 (B). Email: adrian.lewis@fsa.gov.uk
APPOINTMENTS/RE-APPTS SECRETARY: Paul Stanley, 12 Southwold Close, Aylesbury, Bucks, HP21 7EZ. Tel: 01296 580138 (H), 07887 870045 (M), 01869 256019 (B). Email: paul.stanley70@ntlworld.com
EXCHANGE APPOINTMENTS SECRETARY: Simon Cook, Provost Edge, Valley Road, Hughenden Valley, High Wycombe, Buckinghamshire, HP14 4LG. Tel: 01494 565277 (H), 07879 890870 (M), 0118 918 5716 (B). Email: simon.cook@entegria.com
ASSESSMENTS & GRADING: Malcolm Jamieson, Brookfield, St Christophers Close, Little Kingshill, Bucks, HP16 0DU. Tel: 01494 864352 (H), 07850 905732 (M), 01494 488750 (B). Email: mandjjamieson@clara.net
SADO: Adrian Saunders, 19 Redgrave Place, Marlow, Bucks, SL7 1JZ. Tel: 01628 486745 (H). Email: rugby@adriansaunders.plus.com
COUNTY REP: Rodney Hills, 124 Roberts Ride, Hazelmere, High Wycombe, Bucks, HP15 7AN. Tel: 01494 716932 (H), 01628 890464 (B). Email: rodneyhills@yahoo.co.uk

Oxfordshire – 1932

PRESIDENT: Roger Hancock, Sugarswell Bungalow, Shenington, Banbury, OX15 6HW. Tel: 01295 670368 (H), 07932 080374 (M), 01295 270200 (B). Fax: 01295 271874. Email: roger@sugarswell.freeserve.co.uk
SADO: Mike Knight, 49 Sinclair Avenue, Banbury, Oxon, OX16 7BG. Tel: 01295 277752 (H). Email:

mjk@oxref.fsnet.co.uk
SECRETARY: Terry Mallarky, 9 Maule Close, Bloxham, Oxon, OX15 4TR. Tel: 01295 720316. Email:
orfu-admin@dropline.demon.co.uk/terrymallarky@hotmail.com
FINANCE: Clark Friend, 45 Stanway Road, Oxford, OX3 9HU. Tel: 01865 762546 (H)
ASSISTANT TREASURER: Keith Cannock, 31 Cowleaze, Thame, Oxon, OX9 4TB. Tel: 01844 353181
RECRUITMENT & COACHING: Geoff Fitzgerald, Old Tara Barn, Dry Sanford, Oxon, OX13 6JP. Tel:
01865 390797. Email: geoff@techno-research.com
T&D MANAGER: Brian Bumpass, 8 Willow Walk, Wantage, Oxon, OX12 9EN. Tel: 01235 223111 (H).
Email: brian.bumpass@ntlworld.com
APPTS/RE APPTS SECRETARY (WEEKENDS): Ken Bumpass, 39 Woodley Close, Abingdon, Oxon,
OX14 1YJ. Tel: 01235 200137 (H). Email: ken.bumpass@ntlworld.com
APPTS SECRETARY (MIDWEEK): Keith Latham, 29 Churchill Way, Long Hanborough, Witney, OX29
8JJ. Tel: 01993 881985 (H), 07967 206098 (M). Email: keith.latham@tinyworld.co.uk
MEDIA: 6 Culham Close, Abingdon, OX14 2AS. Tel: 01235 533568

Hampshire – 1936
CHAIRMAN/PR: Simon Thomas, 40 Telegraph Lane, Four Marks, Alton, GU34 5AX. Tel: 01420
561552 (H), 07887 873999 (M), 02078 032318 (B). Email: simonthomasuk@yahoo.com
SECRETARY: Eric Smith, 1 Osborne Close, Alton, Hampshire, GU34 1QT. Tel: 01420 544161 (H).
Email: ericsmith@ukgateway.net
FINANCE: Richard Showan, 10 Romsey Road, Eastleigh, SO50 9AL. Tel: 07768 361325 (H), 07768
361325 (M), 02380 614555 (B). Email: rdlshowan@aol.com
RECRUITMENT: John Crocker, 12 Sherfield Close, Bournemouth, Dorset, BH8 0NT. Tel: 01202 530380
(H) 07770 732419 (M), 02380 234345 (B). Email: lynnem@clara.co.uk
T&D OFFICER/DEVELOPMENT REFEREE TRAINER: Paul Burton, 49 Watersmeet, Fareham, PO16
0TG. Tel: 01329 827765 (H), 07967 750203 (M), 02392 765193 (B). Email: paul.rachel@virgin.net
SOCIETY REFEREE TRAINER/NATIONAL FOUNDATION: Dave Hayward, 4 Rowlands Avenue,
Waterlooville, PO7 7RY. Tel: 02392 265697 (H), 02392 568881 (B). Email: 8hayward@uk.ibm.com
MINI/MIDI TRAINER: John Gregory, St Helens, 58 Merrivlae Road, Hillsea, Portsmouth, PO2 0TL.
Tel: 02392 677957 (H), 07799 151710 (M&B). Email: geoff@paiceg.fsnet.co.uk
APPOINTMENTS SECRETARY (WEEKENDS/MIDWEEK): Geoff Paice, 19 Chalcrafts, Alton, GU34
2HD. Tel: 01420 543924 (H), 01420 404032 (B). Email: geoff@paiceg.fsnet.co.uk
RE-APPOINTMENTS SECRETARY (MIDWEEK): Paul Hobby, 8 Kingsmead Avenue, Stubbington,
Fareham, PO14 2NL. Tel: 01329 315388 (H), 07909 803413 (M), 02380 247558 (B). Email:
paulann@hobbyp.freeserve.co.uk
RE-APPOINTMENTS SECRETARY (WEEKENDS): Dave Davies, 13 Montague Road, North End,
Portsmouth, PO2 0ND. Tel: 02392 668275 (H). Email: dave.oldies@virgin.net
DISCIPLINE: Peter Topham, Timbuck, Nett Road, Shrewton, Salisbury, Wiltshire, SP3 4HB. Tel: 01980
620539 (H), 07752 380446 (M). Fax: 01980 620539. Email: peter@topham971.freeserve.co.uk
ASSESSMENT & GRADING/SADO: Jim Firth, 36 Columbine Road, Kempshott Down, Basingstoke,
RG22 5RW. Tel: 01256 327526 (H). Email: james.firth2@btopenworld.com

SOUTH WEST PENINSULAR FEDERATION

CHAIRMAN/APPOINTMENTS/SWAG: Terry Friend, 9 Landulph Gardens, St Budeaux, Plymouth, PL5
1PP. Tel: 01752 360148 (H). Email: trf@fclnet.com
SECRETARY: Barrie Gledhill, 6 Beaumaris Gardens, Hartley, Plymouth, PL3 5LQ. Tel: 01752 308539
(H), 07769 722363 (M). Email: barriegledhill@yahoo.co.uk
FINANCE: John Scott, 11 Tuxton Close, Plympton, Plymouth, Pl7 1QH. Tel: 01752 330840 (H). Email:
johnrscott@tinyworld.co.uk
T&D MANAGER: Steve Harland, 78 Grantley Gardens, Mannamead, Plymouth, PL3 5BS. Tel: 01752 663622
(H), 07710 416852 (M), 01752 836942 (B). Email: steveharland@rfu.com/steve.harland@btinternet.com
APPTS SECRETARY/RE-APPTS SECRETARY: Terry Friend, 59 Peters Park Close, St. Budeaux,

Plymouth PL5 1PP. Tel: 01752 360148 (H). Email: trf@fclnet.com

MODS REP/ADVISER OFFICER: Vaughan Hosking, 11 Orbec Avenue, Kingsteignton, Newton Abbot, Devon TQ12 3ED. Tel: 01626 364781 (H), 07976 804623 (M). Email: kvhosking@aol.com

REPRESENTATIVES: John Sumnall, Seacroft, Cocks Hill, Perranporth, Cornwall, TR6 0AU. Tel: 01872 572788. Email: johnsumnall@btinternet.com

Ian Hamilton, West End Cottage, Main Road, Ashton, Helston, Cornwall, TR13 9SR. Tel: 01736 763594 (H), 07793 211763 (M). Email: biggsyhamilton@msn.com

Cornwall – 1903

PRESIDENT: Phil Allen, 'Meneth Gwyn', High Trewidden Road, The Belyars, St. Ives, TR26 2DP. Tel: 01736 796332 (H). Email: philallen@clodgyview.fsnet.co.uk

David Martin, Treverbyn Rise, Penryn, Cornwall, TR10 8RA. Tel: 01326 372956 (H). Email: dave-martin@eurobell.co.uk

CHAIRMAN/APPTS SEC (WEEKENDS): Ian Hamilton, West End Cottage, Main Road, Ashton, Helston, Cornwall, TR13 9SR. Tel: 01736 763594 (H), 07793 211763 (M). Email: biggsyhamilton@msn.com

SECRETARY/PR/DISCIPLINE: Terry Mortimore, 32 Newbridge Way, Truro, Cornwall, TR1 3LX. Tel: 01872 225827 (H), 07903 315305 (M). Email: terrymortimorecrrs@btopenworld.com

FINANCE: David Driver, 11 Roseland Crescent, Chacewater, Truro, Cornwall, TR4 8JU. Tel: 01872 560676 (H). Email: daviddriver5@netel.net.uk

RECRUITMENT/RETENTION/T&D MANAGER: David May, 12 Carrallack Park, St Just, Penzance, TR19 7UL. Tel: 01736 788285 (H). Email: daisy.may1@btinternet.com

15-A-SIDE/MINI-MIDI TRAINER: Mike Bratt. Tel: 07764 960380 (M), 01872 324661 (B). Fax: 01872 324334. Email: mikebratt@rfu.com

RE-APPTS/APPTS SECRETARY (MIDWEEK): Peter Nichols, Lowenac Hotel, Bassett Road, Camborne, Cornwall, TR14 8SL. Tel: 01209 713635 (H), 01209 713635 (B)

ASSESSMENT & GRADING: John Sumnall, Seacroft, Cocks Hill, Perranporth, Truro, Cornwall, TR6 0AU. Email: johnsumnall@btinternet.com

OTHER VICE CHAIRMAN: Andy Watts, 10 Lelant Meadows, Lelant, TR26 3JS. Email: andywatts@pandamonium.fsworld.co.uk

Devon – 1893

PRESIDENT: Charlie Wakeman, 2 Edwinstowe, Higher Warberry Road, Torquay, TQ1 1SF. Tel: 01803 291384. Email: devonref@yahoo.com

VICE PRESIDENT: Steve Harland, 78 Grantley Gardens, Mannamead, Plymouth, PL3 5BP. Tel: 01752 663622. Email: steve.harland@btinternet.com

SECRETARY: Tom Healy, 16 Venn Grove, Hartley, Plymouth, PL3 5PG. Tel: 01752 796173 (H). Email: tomhealy.rugby@blueyonder.co.uk

FINANCE: Mike Harrison, 'Sequoia' George Nympton, South Molton, North Devon, EX36 4JE. Tel: 01769 579032 (H). Email: mikeharrison@dunbanking.fsnet.co.uk

T&D MANAGER: David Hinshelwood, 'Tahini', Kerswell, Cullompton, Devon, EX15 2EJ. Tel: 01884 266500 (H), 07974 656587 (M). Email: dhinshelwood@farming.co.uk

APPTS SECRETARY(MIDWEEK/WEEKENDS): Peter Webb, Glebe Cottage, Weech Road, Dawlish, EX7 9BW. Tel: 01626 862800 (H). Email: peter.j.webb@btinternet.com

RE-APPTS SECRETARY: Alan Meagor, Fields View, 28 Greenover Road, Brixham, TQ5 9LY. Tel: 01803 859722 (H). Email: alan.meagor@btopenworld.com

DISCIPLINE: Tim Rice, 48 Aller Park Road, Newton Abbot, TQ12 4NQ. Tel: 01626 335120

ASSESSMENT & GRADING/SADO: Vaughan Hosking, 11 Orbec Avenue, Kingsteignton, Newton Abbot, TQ12 3ED. Tel: 01626 364781 (H). Email: kvhosking@aol.com

EXCHANGE SECRETARY: Terry Friend, 59 Peter's Park Close, St Budeaux, Plymouth, PL5 1PP. Tel: 01752 360148 (H). Email: trf@fclnet.com

ELECTED ACTIVE MEMBER: Paddy Dummett, 9 Cottey Brook, Tiverton, EX16 5BR. Tel: 01884 242755. Email: paddydummett@hotmail.com

Plymouth – 1927
PRESIDENT: Trevor Hunter, 78 Shirburn Road, Eggbuckland, Plymouth, PL6 5PH. Tel: 01752 510056 (H). Email: tjflag@aol.com
CHAIRMAN/RECRUITMENT & RETENTION: Alan Mansell, 81 Elburton Road, Elburton, Plymouth, PL9 8JL. Tel: 01752 408710 (H). Email: alanmansell@blueyonder.co.uk
SECRETARY/PR: John Scott, 11 Tuxton Close, Plympton, Plymouth PL7 1QH. Tel: 01752 330840 (H), 07721 437648 (M), 01404 821500 (B). Fax: 01752 318947. Email: johnrscott@tinyworld.co.uk
FINANCE: Ken Hamblin, 110 Pemros Road, St. Budeaux, Plymouth, PL5 1NG. Tel: 01752 365404 (H)
T&D MANAGER: Steve Harland, 78 Grantley Gardens, Mannamead, Plymouth, PL3 5BP. Tel: 01752 663622 (H), 07710 416852 (M). Email: steve.harland@btinternet.com
APPTS SECRETARY/RE-APPOINTMENTS: Ken Dobson, 6 Belle Vue Road, Hooe, Plymouth, PL9 9NR. Tel: 01752 406229 (H), 01803 677139 (B). Fax: 01752 406229. Email: daddyref@btinternet.com
DISCIPLINE: Devon RFU Disciplinary Committee, The Dartmoor Lodge, Peartree Cross, Ashburton, Devon. Tel: 01364 652232
ASSESSMENT & GRADING/SADO: Bob Anstis, 33 Frensham Avenue, Glenholt, Plymouth, PL6 7JW. Tel: 01752 709706 (H). Email: ranstizz@aol.com
OTHER: John Steell, 17 Side Close, Staddiscombe, Plymouth, PL9 9VQ. Tel: 01752 492090 (H), 07732 673483 (M)

GLOUCESTERSHIRE ASSOCIATION OF RUGBY UNION REFEREES

CHAIRMAN: Clive Annetts, The Mount, Ashleworth, Gloucester, GL19 4JH. Tel: 01452 700870 (H). Email: cliveannetts@aol.com
VICE CHAIRMAN: Ian Woodgate, 119 Wemberham Lane, Yatton, Bristol, BS49 4BP. Tel: 01934 834761 (H), 07976 313996 (M). Fax: 01934 832836. Email: ian.woodgate@btinternet.com
SECRETARY: Alan White, 60 Hartlebury Way, Charlton Kings, Gloucester, GL52 6YB. Tel: 01242 239448 (H). Email: alanewhite@btopenworld.com
FINANCE: David Cook, Westway School Lane, Barrow Gurney, Somerset, BS48 3RZ. Tel: 01275 472406 (H)
SOCIETY REP FOR GLOUCESTER: Adrian Stephenson, 10 Brookside Villas, Barnwood, Gloucester, GL2 0SS. Tel: 01452 531793 (H), 07787 531717 (M), 01452 712424 x 1893 (B). Email: ade.stephenson@messier-dowty.com
T&D MANAGER: David Payne, Parkside, The Park, Minchinhampton, Gloucester, GL6 9EQ. Tel: 01453 884334 (H). Email: dave-janet@parkside100.freeserve.co.uk
SADO: Tim Mahoney, 3 Beech Mount Grove, Hengrove, Bristol, BS14 9DN. Tel: 01275 541228 (H). Email: mahoneytp@aol.com/tim.mahoney@jobcentreplus.gsi.gov.uk

Bristol – 1893
CHAIRMAN: Ian Woodgate, 119 Wemberham Lane, Yatton, Bristol, BS49 4BP. Tel: 01934 834761 (H), 07976 313996 (M). Fax: 01934 832836. Email: ian.woodgate@btinternet.com
SECRETARY: Ivor Sobey, 6 Branksome Crescent, Filton, Bristol, BS34 7EQ. Tel: 0117 983 6879 (H), 0117 982 8743 (B). Fax: 0117 982 5706 (B). Email: ivor_sobey@ryder.com
FINANCE: David Cook, Westway, School Lane, Barrow Gurney, Bristol BS48 3RZ. Tel: 01275 472406 (H)
RECRUITMENT & RETENTION OFFICER/T.O/COACH: Richard Potterton , 41 Stoke Lane, Westbury-on-Trym, Bristol, BS9 3DW. Tel: 0117 962 3927 (H), 0117 923 3815 (M). Email: Richard.potterton@lloydstsb.co.uk
PR OFFICER: Jane Deane, 3 Beechmount Grove, Hengrove, Bristol, BS14 9DN. Tel: 0117 933 2519 (H). Email: janepdeane@aol.com
APPTS SECRETARY (WEEKENDS): Geoff Warren, 45 Bridgwater Road, Uplands, Bristol. BS13 7AX. Tel: 0117 987 7637 (H), 07798 517469 (M), 0117 934 1045 (B). Email: geoffwarren@bristolwater.co.uk
APPTS SECRETARY (SUNDAY): Les Brunyee, 43 Millmead House, Silcox Avenue, Hartcliffe, Bristol, BS13 0JN. Tel: 0117 964 4685 (H), 07946 585265 (M&B)

APPOINTMENTS SECRETARY: Bob Mole. Tel: 07949 753620 (M). Fax: 07092 316247. Email: bob_mole@moler-wwp.co.uk

RE-APPTS SECRETARY: Chris Watts. Tel: 07786 262230 (M)

ASSESSMENT & GRADING OFFICER: Gerry Weatherhead, 48 Beach Avenue, Severn Beach, Bristol, BS35 4BP. Tel: 01454 631636 (H&B)

SADO: Tim Mahoney, 3 Beechmount Grove, Hengrove, Bristol, BS14 9DN. Tel: 0117 933 2519 (H). Email: mahoneytp@aol.com/ tim.mahoney@jobcentreplus.gsi.gov.uk

Gloucester & District – 1895

PRESIDENT: Tony Roberts, 51 Gambier Parry Gardens, Gloucester, GL2 9RD. Tel: 01452 307735 (H), 01452 425654 (B), 07803 602871 (M). Email: tony.roberts@gloucestershire.gov.uk

CHAIRMAN: Clive Annetts, The Mount, Ashleworth, Gloucester, GL19 4JH. Tel: 01452 700870 (H). Email: cliveannetts@aol.com

VICE-CHAIRMAN/ADVISOR DEVELOPMENT & REPORTS: David Payne, Parkside, The Park, Minchinhampton, Gloucester, GL6 9EQ. Tel: 01453 884334 (H), 07786 103114 (M). Email: dave-janet@parkside100.freserve.com.uk/davidpayne@ruf.com

SECRETARY/DISCIPLINE: Alan White, 60 Hartlebury Way, Charlton Kings, Gloucester, GL52 6YB. Tel: 01242 239448 (H). Email: alanewhite@btopenworld.com

FINANCE: Les Newcombe, 41 Mayfield Drive, Hucclecote, Gloucester, GL3 3DS. Tel: 01452 614886 (H). Email: dasherathome@hotmail.com

T&D MANAGER: Alan Biggs, 80 Haywards Road, Charlton Kings, Cheltenham, GL52 6RJ. Tel: 01242 510173 (H), 07789 001694 (M). Email: abbr20876@blueyonder.co.uk

APPOINTMENTS SECRETARY: Rodger Brennan, Driftwood, Shutter Lane, Gotherington, Gloucester, GL52 9EZ. Tel: 01242 678308 (H), 07989 974633 (M). Email: rmcb1915@driftwood60.freeserve.co.uk

TRAINING ADMINISTRATOR: Arthur Grun, The Pines, 29 The Street, Shipton Mayne, Gloucester, GL8 8PN. Tel: 01666 880487 (H), 07802 211773 (M). Email: acfgrun@aol.com

INDUCTION OFFICER: Colin Reeves, 186 Barnwood Road, Gloucester, GL4 3JZ. Tel: 01452 610161 (H), 01452 428357 (B). Email: ccatsgmr@ukgateway.net

ADVISOR CO-ORDINATOR: 10 Hallas House, Holywell Road, Malvern, Worcester, WR14 6LE. Tel: 01684 562380 (H). Fax: 01905 756700. Email: peterlewis@fslife.co.uk

MEMBERS REPRESENTATIVE: Adrian Stephenson, 10 Brookside Villas, Barnwood, Gloucester, GL2 0SS. Tel: 01452 531793 (H), 07787 531717 (M), 01452 712424 x 1893 (B). Email: ade.stephenson@messier-dowty.org

EXCHANGE APPOINTMENTS: David Meek, Trilia House, The Cross, Drybrook, GL17 9EB. Tel: 01594 541287 (H). Email: dave@meek85.fsnet.co.uk

SUNDAY APPOINTMENTS: Phil Harrison, 141 Victoria House, Bradmore, Wolverhampton, WV3 7HA. Tel: 01902 334237 (H), 07958 658963 (M), 01743 850391 (B). Email: thehead@grafton.shropshire.sch.uk

WEBMASTER: Peter Shortell, 81 Hales Road, Cheltenham, GL52 6SR. Tel: 01242 510849 (H). Email: pshortell@bigfoot.com

EDITOR: Dean & Simon Griffiths, 10 College Fileds, Longlevens, Gloucetser, GL2 0AG. Tel: 01452 532638. Email: dean@dg-systems-uk.co.uk

WESSEX FEDERATION

CHAIRMAN: TBA

ADMINISTRATOR: Alan Avery, 24 Wetherby Close, Milborne St. Andrew, Blandford, Dorset, DT11 0JN. Tel: 01258 837450 (H). Email: alanavery@bournemouth-net.co.uk

REFEREE UNION REPRESENTATIVE: Dave Thomas, 53 Somerset Avenue, Taunton, TA1 5HX. Tel: 01823 322058 (H). Email: djt.somersetave@virgin.net

REPRESENTATIVE ON SWAG: Dave Smith, 13 Queens Close, Sutton Benger, Chippenham, SN15 4SB. Tel: 01249 720602 (H), 01666 823201 (B)

DEVELOPMENT & TRAINING: Somerset – TBA

Dorset & Wilts – Richard Shore, 4 Kingsley Close, Bournemouth, Dorset BH6 4JQ. Tel: 01202 426524 (H). Email: shore.rg@virgin.net

APPOINTMENTS & ADVISING: Somerset – TBA

Dorset & Wilts – Stephen Dowse, Tregirls, 179 East Gomldon Road, Salisbury, SP4 6NB. Tel: 01980 619313. Email: dowse@sdowse.fsnet.co.uk

Dorset & Wilts – 1953

CHAIRMAN: Robin Miller, 18 Tanyard Lane, Shaftsbury, Dorset, SP7 8HW. Tel: 01747 854765 (H). Email: robin.miller@btopenworld.com

SECRETARY: Alan Avery, 24 Wetherby Close, Milborne St. Andrew, Blandford, Dorset, DT11 0JN. Tel: 01258 837450 (H). Email: alanavery@bournemouth-net.co.uk

TREASURER: Bill Byham, Humbrook, Mill Lane, Broughton Gifford, Melksham, Wilts, SN12 8NY. Tel: 01225 782441 (H)

DORSET ORGANISER: Geoff Worrall, 56 High Street, Wincanton, Somerset, BA9 9JF. Tel: 01963 32503 (H), 07885 776477 (M). Email: gsworrall@aol.com

WILTSHIRE ORGANISER: Eric Bullion, Grafton Edge, Common Road, Malmesbury, Wiltshire. Tel: 01666 826740 (H). Email: home@graftonedge.fsnet.co.uk

EXCHANGE SECRETARY: Marc Young, 25 Vicarage Road, Netheravon, Salisbury, Wiltshire, SP4 9RW: Email: marc@myoung254.freeserve.co.uk

GRADING SECRETARY/SADO: Stephen Dowse, Tregirls, 179 East Gomeldon Road, Salisbury, Wiltshire, SP4 6NB. Tel: 01980 619054 (H), 01980 673345 (B). Email: dowse@sdowse.fsnet.co.uk

T&D MANAGER: Richard Shore, 4 Kingsley Close, Bournemouth, Dorset BH6 4JQ. Tel: 01202 426524 (H). Email: shore.rg@virgin.net

RECRUITMENT/PR OFFICER: Gwyn Allsopp, 131 Sandy Lane, Upton, Poole, Dorset, BH15 5LT. Tel: 01202 625626 (H), 07770 924448 (M). Email: gwyn@gallsopppoole.fsnet.co.uk

Somerset – 1889

CHAIRMAN/DISCIPLINE: Dave Thomas, 53 Somerset Avenue, Taunton, TA1 5HX. Tel: 01823 322058 (H). Email: djt.somersetave@virgin.net

SECRETARY: Graeme King, 13 Staddlestones, Midsomer Norton, Somerset, BA3 2PP. Tel: 01761 417827 (H), 01761 413869 (B). Fax: 01761 414131. Email: graeme@kingwatkins.co.uk

FINANCE: Peter Miles, The Garden Flat, 29 Daniel Street, Bath, BA2 9AD. Tel: 01225 462515

RECRUITMENT & RETENTION/VICE CHAIRMAN: Mel Hilman, 64 Plantagenet Chase, Yeovil, Somerset, BA20 2PR. Tel: 01935 429032 (H)

T&D MANAGER: Kevin Obern, Valley View, Chilcompton, Somerset, BA3 4EN. Tel: 01761 233013 (H), 01761 409234 (B). Email: k.obern@btinternet.com

APPTS SECRETARY (WEEKENDS): Dave Smith, 13 Queens Close, Sutton Benger, Chippenham, Wilts, SN15 4SB. Tel: 01249 720602 (H), 01666 823201 (B), 07778 236666 (M). Email: thirteenqueensclose@btinternet.com

APPTS SECRETARY (MIDWEEK): Clive Rees, 216 The Butts, Frome, BA11 4AG. Tel: 01373 461050 (H)

RE-APPTS SECRETARY: Mike Purse, 30 High Street, Hinton Charterhouse, Bath, BA3 6AN. Tel: 01225 722836 (H). Fax: 01225 722866

Harry Vince, 5 Tiley Close, Keynsham, Bristol, BS18 1NX. Tel: 0117 986 4094 (H). Email: H.vince@btinternet.com

ASSESSMENT & GRADING: Tony Pomeroy, Hafod-y-Gan, Newton Road, North Petherton, Somerset, TA6 6SN. Tel: 01278 662181 (H), 07976 518773 (M). Fax: 01278 662178. Email: pomeroyhome@aol.com